Leading Children

Written by
Penny Frank and Nick Harding

Designed and edited by
David Payne, Eileen Turner and Jane Gibbs

Published by St John's Extension Studies, Bramcote, NOTTINGHAM NG9 3RL

© St John's Extension Studies, 1998, 2001. New edition 2005, revised and reprinted 2009.

Photographs from Morguefile (http://www.morguefile.com) are royalty free.

Printed and bound by B & B Press Ltd., Rotherham

ISBN 978-1-900920-13-1

Contents

Who is this course for?

This workbook is for people who want to understand more about the leadership of children and to be more effective in it. They will probably be involved in leading children already. But they may be looking at the leadership of children for the first time – either because they have moved into a different church situation, or because they have suddenly been given that responsibility in the absence of anyone else.

It is unfortunate that many local churches think that anyone can lead children. This is not true. Leading children involves specific gifts which are not held by everyone. The leadership gifts of understanding the Bible, the ability to explain it to others, the gifts of faith, prayer, tenacity and patience are all needed. But for leaders of children we must add: an enjoyment of the company of children, a fascination with the way they think and feel, a longing for children to enter into a relationship with God.

Along with the spiritual gifts there are many practical ones which are needed. A leader of children needs to be organised, a good communicator, able to accept a certain amount of mess and noise. They need to be ready to learn from children as well as being confident about the faith they want to teach. Above all they should be someone who is excited by what they see God doing in their own life, the life of their church and community, as well as in the lives of children.

That can feel overwhelming! But as long as you enjoy the company of children and have a relationship with Jesus Christ, then you are on the starting line. If you recognise any or all of these gifts as your own, then this course is for you.

The leadership of children is fundamental to any society or community. The church is no exception. If the church ignores children and fails to provide for their leadership, the church itself is impoverished. It will not receive a child's wisdom and perception, which is so different from any adult. It will reject the gift of a child's faith, which is unique. If the church fails to lead children well, it will also be failing to grow leadership skills in children – the new generation of leaders. This means that the present dearth of leadership in the church can only get worse in the next generation.

This course aims to help you examine your own gifts in the leadership of children, and to grow them. It takes the work which each of us does in our own communities and sets that in the big context of all that God longs to do in the lives of children today. And it challenges you to consider not simply those children already in the church but those who have yet to be invited to enter a new life with Christ.

How to use this course

If you have received this course material in a loose-leaf file it is likely that you have registered with St John's Extension Studies and are intending to complete all the assignments and have them marked by a tutor. In that case you can ignore the rest of this page and start working now!

If you have received this material in book form you may have thought of it as a useful resource but have no expectation of treating it as a 'course'. You might find the following paragraphs useful.

The book is designed not only to give you information but to help you grow in your ability to lead children in the Christian faith. You can use it in a number of ways:

On your own

This is not ideal, but if it is the only practical way for you to work with the material, you can still benefit from it. The key is to make sure you learn to reflect on your experiences of working with children as well as doing the practical tasks. Just reading this book is not likely to move you on significantly in your ability to lead children.

With others

If a few of you use the workbook together, you will learn a lot from each other – other people will see in you things you can't see yourself. Remember to be honest with each other; this will help you all learn more. You can do the practical experience things together or separately, and come together to talk them through.

As part of a local training system

The workbook can be used by an experienced leader of children to train others. You may know of suitable people with experience and knowledge who could work with a group to help you move forward.

As part of a course

If you have not yet registered for the St John's Extension Studies course you can do so now! This combines distance learning with access to a weekend training event, and draws on the knowledge of experienced children's leaders as tutors. This level of training is for anyone who wants to develop their leadership skills, including those who may head up the children's work at their own church. Students who complete the unit successfully can offer it as part of the St John's Certificate in Christian Studies.

There are many other organisations who can advise about children's work (Scripture Union, CPAS, Children's Ministry, Anglican dioceses etc). Many organise training days. If you register for the St John's distance learning course we hope you will attend a training event some time during your studies.

St John's Extension Studies
Bramcote, Nottingham NG9 3RL

0115 925 1117

ext.studies@stjohns-nottm.ac.uk

www.stjohns-nottm.ac.uk

Who'd be a children's leader?

This unit is about the kinds of people that make good children's leaders. It also introduces the aims of this workbook and prepares you for what will be involved in undertaking it as a course.

Contents

Am I the type?

I am doing children's work because there was no-one else. Now I feel the need to do it better.

Children have changed such a lot, and I want to keep in touch.

My own children hate church, so I thought I'd get involved to try to change things.

My church leader told me to do more study about kid's work. This could be the answer

I don't have much time to study...I'm too busy preparing for Sunday.

I've realised that if the church has any future it needs to have children now!

I feel tired and uninspired. I need to be freshened up.

I'm not sure how to do it better, but I want to try.

How can we teach children at church in the way they learn at school?

I only know the way we work with children in my own church.

Tick any of the comments above that make sense to you. Write below how you feel....

Write down why you are looking at this workbook and what is motivating you to find out more....

Write down why you are looking at this workbook and what is motivating you to find out more....

What do they want?

What do you have in your mind as the sort of person your church is looking for to lead a group of 4-6 year olds? Imagine the following appears in your church magazine:

YOU ARE INVITED....

..to become a member of a small but significant leadership team in our church.

Your duties will involve you in membership of a small group of children who are aged between 4 and 6 years old. They will be your responsibility for an hour every Sunday morning to be kept safe and happy, to learn about God and to grow a relationship with him through Jesus Christ.

They will want to explore ways of worshipping him that they can use at home during the week. They will need to see in your life an illustration of what you are teaching them about God.

We are asking you to be committed to this role from September through to July. Please pray...and reply.

It's the spice of life!

A team can be made up of very different people – in fact it is a better team when there is variety. Teams are great when they bring together a huge range of people with many and varied gifts. Although this presents challenges and the possibility of disagreements too, it also makes for great fun and a better service to our children.

It also means that whatever the variety already on a team, there is space for you with your specific gifts and personality. As you work with the others, your gifts will grow and you will learn new skills from them.

Write a list of personal characteristics the 'ideal' worker would need in order to fill that role. Then look at the ideas at the bottom of page 13.

Five people that were

If you gather together

- the teachers and teaching assistants from your local school
- the parents of the children in your church groups
- the people on the children's team in your local church

they would all be different people. The journey they have travelled to their leadership role would be varied and contrasting. Here are some leaders that Penny Frank has worked with ….Are you like any of these?

Mrs Hughes was the head teacher in a local primary school. She was close to retirement but only recently married, had an outrageous sense of humour and a real compassion for the people living in the difficult environment around the school. She was good at growing the individual gifts of her staff, dealt well with the two men on the team, and seemed able to relate to her support staff as easily as to the professionals. She seemed lonely though and occasionally went into the staff room to enjoy the fun – not usual practice in schools and something which some members of the team resented. She was great with parents, who always felt welcomed, but a nightmare to the Local Authority which saw her as a 'law to herself'.

Peter was a grandfather. He had always been in the church and had had five children of his own. Peter had at one time been the Superintendent of the Sunday School, but by the time I came along he wasn't involved at all. When I asked him to lead the group for pre-schoolers he looked as though I had asked him to fly; but after some time to think, he agreed to try one term. He was brilliant! He wasn't good at telling stories or at creative ideas because actually he was too formal, but the children were calm and happy when he was around. He was very practical and down to earth with them – never patronised them nor asked too little of them. He stayed for years and his presence there in Scramblers encouraged a lot of younger men to get involved with small children and not just with the teenagers.

Sue was an experienced and skilful children's leader at her church. She was one of those careful planners who always knew what was happening. She kept a record of our planning meetings, so that if we forgot what was going on we always asked Sue. The children loved her because she was dependable, gently humourous and well-prepared. They knew that if Sue was there, they would have a good morning and enjoy it. The other leaders liked her because they knew she would support them even if what they had planned started to go wrong.

Steve was still at school when he began helping with children's work at our church. The children loved him because he did noisy and fun things. I remember wishing at times that he would be quiet and calm down – I was in the next room behind a partition and it was very noisy at times. But when I think of the way he dramatised Bible stories with them, or taught them energetic songs, or had bright ideas for 'let's do something different morning', I'm really glad that Steve was there.

Ann, Avril and Anthea have all recently offered to help with the children in church. They met each other at the latest Alpha course; they then joined a Home Group and heard about the children's groups. Now they are always full of funny stories over coffee, and they gel the team together. They make others feel it doesn't matter if they make a mess of something, because there is always the basis for a funny story in it. They are as rough-mouthed as the children sometimes and others wince at the things they say, but the children love them and receive a good picture of faith from them.

Draw a sketch of someone you know who leads children's work. How would you describe them?

The wisdom of experience

From many angles

This workbook puts together, as one learning experience

theology

educational principles

ideas for good practice

illustrations from experience

research results

assessable tasks

Although it aims to look at important issues in depth, it does so by approaching each issue through as many openings as possible. This means that the course should be accessible and 'user-friendly' to a wide range of people.

Most of us learn more from what we do, than from what we read and study. It's true for children, and it's true for us as adults too. Reading words and writing them can influence us, but change is far more radical and long-lasting if the process of our learning is more active and creative than that.

Even if you have never read a thing about giving leadership to children, you will still know things about it. You will have some experience in your life to draw on. You have been a child once yourself. You related to other children then, and have done so since. And if you want to know more about relating to children, you can do it partly by broadening that experience which you already have.

Starting from experience

Each Unit in this workbook will start from experience. This is so that as many people as possible will be able to start from what they know. It will help make each Unit accessible.

Some are more experienced with children than others. The beginning of each Unit sets out just how experienced you need to be in order to complete the Unit – and suggests ways of getting that experience if you don't have it already.

You might be able to start straight into a particular Unit because you already have the necessary background experience. For another Unit you may find that you need to do all the preparation exercises suggested. In yet another Unit you may find that you have enough experience to start, and you can do some of the preparation material alongside the work in the Unit itself.

This experience base is very important if we are to engage with children. There will often seem to be quicker and easier ways of 'learning' what is contained in the rest of each Unit, but the approach suggested aims at involving you as a whole person – rather than just your head. You will never engage with children simply through the processes of the mind. Don't rush through the Units and activities, and if something sparks more thinking in you, follow that thought to widen your learning!

The view from below

This workbook aims to look at both sides of each issue – from the adult leader's perspective and from the child's perspective. Strangely, this second perspective is often missed, even when talking about how we help children in matters of faith.

So remember the truth that a child's faith and spirituality is something for which both the child and the leader have responsibility. Children need help in developing their faith but it can't be 'done' to them, and we as leaders can learn from them too.

> What help do you think you will need in completing this course? Write your thoughts here and then look at the next page.

To help you

As you go through this workbook you will need help. It's unrealistic to think that you can develop as a children's leader in glorious isolation. So start by getting the help you need.

1. Someone to work through the book with

This could be someone who is in the same position as you, or someone with more experience who wants to freshen up their thinking. Otherwise find someone to ask you how it is going, encourage you, and spur you on when necessary.

2. Access to a place where children are

Ideally you will need to arrange to be able to make regular observations in another situation before you start following through this workbook. It is not possible to get all the way through successfully without arranging for these observations to take place.

You will be aware of the careful requirements that schools, churches and other organisations have for those who want access to children. You will need to prove your legitimacy to those in charge, be it through a covering letter from your church leader, evidence of appropriate checking (for instance a current Criminal Records Bureau Disclosure) and/or by arranging an introduction to a school, group or church through a friend or colleague.

The ideal place to observe children and follow the course requirements is in a primary school. However, this may not be possible, so there are other options available including after-school activities which are often run by voluntary sector agencies and churches, or visiting and observing on a regular basis the children's groups at another church local to you. Please remember when approaching any of these bodies that you have no right of access, and those in charge will be rightly cautious of granting permission to you without being sure you are an appropriate person to have access to children in their charge. If you plan to take photographs to help you work through this book you will need to check this out, seek permission, and in many cases inform parents. More information on this is given below.

3. Camera

You are encouraged to record your observations. Photographs are a way of recording these, as well as making notes or writing down the results of working with children. It may not be possible for you to take photographs of the children you are observing, or you may be required to seek parental permission before you do so. Please check first! If you are not able to record your observations by photograph draw a sketch, or write a few words that describe the scene. Sketches, descriptions and photographs should all be mounted in this workbook or loose-leaf file to help you reflect on what you saw and what you are learning.

4. Time

Anything worthwhile takes time to accomplish. This workbook will take some of your time regularly if you plan to make worthwhile progress. You may need to talk to your church leader and family about how to find the extra time you'll need.

Each Unit will take you around 5 hours to complete, although the more carefully you work and the more observations you make the more time you'll need. It is important to keep up the momentum in doing the course, so plan a realistic schedule. If you have registered for the course with St John's, you will have been given a Student Guide. This includes a Marks Record on which to write in your target dates – make sure you do, and try to keep to them.

And at the end....

...... you will have discovered that you don't have to leave it to parents and professional teachers to hand on the faith to a new generation. It is a task which can involve you too. You will gain the confidence to explain your faith and to teach the Bible to a generation of people whose culture is different from yours.

And whether you are doing the course to stimulate yourself about a subject you already know a lot about, or to introduce you to new issues, it is there to be enjoyed. Children make everything into a game – and you can too! (Go on ......)

Space for your notes.....

The journey of your life

Elmwich, Sept 15th

Dear Great Aunt Pam,

How did you stick this Sunday School teaching lark for so long? 40 years? I'm not going to survive four Sundays at this rate! I'm exhausted.

The children are brilliant and I think they like me too which is gratifying. I told the story the other week and led the game. They listened really well to the story, but went all over the place in the game. I felt I needed a referee!

But this week I have been asked to re-tell the Bible passage and then explain it to them. How in the world am I supposed to do that? It's the story of the sower and I know it backwards and I could explain it to you because you would know what it meant anyway. But to a group of 4 year olds? Well, they will go all over the place as they did in the game and I will feel really stupid as though I don't under-stand it myself.

I sat down tonight and tried to write out what Jesus said it meant in words they would understand and I think I understand it now better than I did before but . . . .

I'll finish this letter after Sunday and tell you what happens!

We have said already that a child's faith is something for which both the children and adults have responsibility, and is not something which is done to the child.

The children are not the only ones who will benefit from this. It is said that if you cannot explain an issue so that children can understand it, then you probably don't understand the issue properly yourself. The church is very much the poorer for not taking its children seriously. Jesus said something about that somewhere…

As you view things from a child's perspective, you should also expect your own faith and understanding to grow. We can learn from children, and learn from looking at life and faith their way. Learning more about ministry with children is not just:

- to expand your mind
- to make you a better leader
- to carry out more training
- to ensure that you are seen as a valuable member of the team
- to help you make things better for the children you work with

but it is also

- to grow you as a person

This is the best, safest and most exciting way of preparing yourself for the role as a leader of children.

So, working through this workbook should help you grow in understanding of your own faith and your spiritual life too. Please expect and pray for this course to change you. Our hope is that you reach the last page feeling excited that your own faith has been set alight by looking at the faith of children. It is a process of change for the whole of your person.

Become like a child

We can never become a child again, but for many spiritual and practical reasons we must continually try to enter a subject through the door a child might use – and see how different the room looks!

Many of the Units will encourage you to look back at your own experience as a child. This is not because every 6 year old or every 9 year old is the same. Nor because the world is the same now as when you were a child. Obviously neither of these things is true. But as we look back, we will find that God uses our own childhood memories to give insight and illustration to what we are learning and considering.

My Thoughts (The 'ideal' leader, from page 5)

Have you described someone who is beyond the skills of the Angel Gabriel? An individual leader has some characteristics and skills, and across the team you would hope to have the lot! The team would consist of those who are good at reassuring unhappy children, others who are good at organisation, and others who are confident to tell stories or lead games. There will be some who are in daily contact with children, and some who are nervous of them. You may like laughing, or singing, or talking, or loving people – the two vital qualities are that you love God through Jesus Christ and you enjoy being with children.

5 good reasons

There are many reasons why children's leaders keep going after many years in such a challenging role. Here are some reasons why they stick it out:

But I love messing around with glue and glitter and everyone else would think I was mad if I did it!

Working in a team of people on this long term project of evangelism among unchurched children has been wonderful – I've laughed until my sides have ached!

Where else do I receive the unconditional love which those children give me!

But I wouldn't give up for anything – it really disciplines me to study God's Word and to struggle with the hard bits!

I have seen God work more overtly with children than I ever have seen in a group of adults – it's brilliant!

Try it for yourself!

Talk to two or three people you know who are children's leaders – either in church or in local schools. What would they say about why they work with children? Write down what they say in the bubbles:

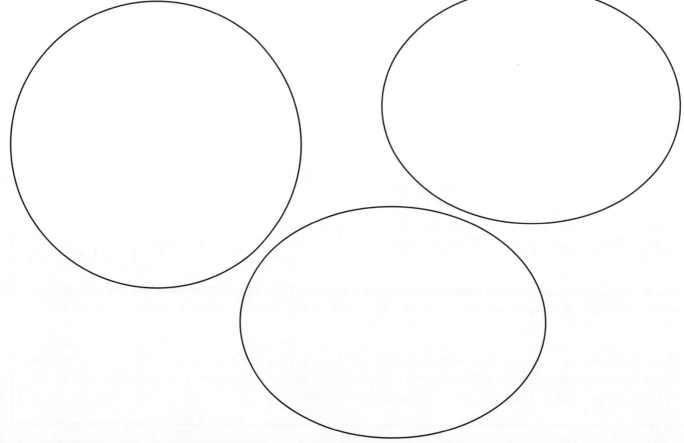

Is this what you want?

Then children's leadership is for you. And it will be one of the most rewarding experiences you ever have.

This is an experience you will have in partnership with the child. The children in your group do not have to 'buy in' to that partnership. They will teach you and influence you without ever being aware of doing so. But you need to buy into it because in a very real sense you will be changed – never to be the same again.

> Where do you feel your Christian life needs to change? Can you see ways in which doing work with children may actually help you in this? Write them down.

Check it out

Look down this checklist. If you can answer 'Yes' to at least three of these items, then this course will be a good use of your time and energy. Start it with confidence – and enthusiasm.

☐ Are you an experienced leader who would like the opportunity to take stock of what you are doing and how you are doing it?

☐ Are you a new leader who would like the opportunity to understand what you have taken on and to start to grow into leadership?

☐ Would you like to learn more about the theology of children – how God sees them and communicates with us about them in the Bible?

☐ Do you feel out of touch with the world children live in, the way they learn and think and respond?

☐ Would you like to be confident to grow children in their faith and spirituality, so that they enjoy God's company now and start to grow characteristics of leadership themselves?

☐ Would you like to be more confident as you prepare the Bible material to teach your group each week?

☐ Are you concerned to understand more about how the family background of the children in your group affects the way in which they are developing and responding?

☐ Do you want to enjoy your leadership more?

☐ Do you want to be more confident of the contribution you can make to the life of the rest of the church community as the leader of children?

☐ Do you want to look forward to the times when your group meets rather than being glad when it is over?

☐ = my score out of 10

The natural child

This Unit establishes a strong pattern of observation and reflection which you will use throughout this course. It also introduces the concept of child development, in the various areas that make up a child's life.

Contents

Getting into it!

In order for this Unit to be effective, you need to have some previous experience and knowledge of children. A knowledge of child development only has impact where there is experience and knowledge of children to form a framework for it.

This framework has two main aspects:

---

1. A living,
day-by-day
gut-level
empathy with children

Once you get into the habit of empathising with children, the knowledge of the patterns of their development will cause you to say 'Ah yes!' When you say this, you are recognising a pattern which is actually already familiar to you but for which you now have a 'label'. This label makes you more aware of it and helps you to think about it.

In this way you are able to understand:

- which of the patterns you have seen in one five year old in your group is particular to them – an individual pattern

- which tendencies are patterns which you might expect to see in many five year olds – a typical pattern.

Both patterns are important in the work we do.

- The first reminds us that we must treat every child as an individual.

- The second enables us to grow more skilled in our role as these typical patterns become familiar to us.

In order to boost your basic feel for children, I want you to embark on six hours of child observation. This will saturate your mind with them and heighten your awareness of them. Here are some tips for getting the most out of those six hours.

Basic preparation

Look at the schools, families and church groups available in your community and decide which would be the best place for your six hours of child observation. Then:

- Approach the parent, leader or teacher

- Explain clearly what you wish to do

- Show them this section of the workbook

- Allow time for them to check child protection regulations, CRB checks etc

- Ask to come for a preparatory visit to become recognised by the children

- Fix clear dates and times for your observations

- Stick to agreed times as much as possible

Preparatory visit

Go on a preliminary visit for at least half an hour. Take with you the observation sheet (see page 22) so that the leader can see what sort of things you are looking for. Choose with her or him the best place for you to use for observation – this may be static or a 'joining in' member of the group. Neither of these is 'best' – it is really your personal preference. You may want to try both and decide in which role you are most observant.

Have questions in mind

On your first visit ask yourself these basic questions:

- Which child do I notice most – and why?

- Which child is most easily overlooked – and why?

- Was I most aware of noise/quiet, movement/stillness, children/adults, people/objects?

- What emotions can I see in the group – anger, joy, humour, affection, impatience?

- How do children arrive – and leave?

Focus on one child

On your subsequent visits choose one child to observe. Build up a picture of the child over the five hours. Each time take this list of questions and add to your observations. Remember that you are not expected to have direct contact with that individual child or single him/her out for special attention. This would cause concern from the responsible adults.

- How does the child react to becoming a member of the group?

- How does the child respond to other children?

- How does the child respond to adults?

- What questions does the child ask?

- What emotions does the child show?

- What does the child like?

- What does the child dislike?

- What makes the child laugh?

- What do you find attractive about the child?

- What do you find unattractive about the child?

2. The experience of being a children's leader

You may think "But I thought that this course would make me into a leader!" Well, it will certainly help but a course will not make you a leader of children in the absence of experience with children.

So one of the requirements before you start this Unit is that you have had six months of regular child leadership contact. If you have not had this before, you need to embark on it now.

At your church, work with children may operate on a rota, so each leader has child leadership contact only one week in three or four. 'Six months regular child leadership contact' means that you go on that rota every week for six months.

Or, in your children's work, you may have 'leaders' and 'helpers'. You may wonder which you are supposed to be. That's a difficult question to answer without knowing how leaders and helpers are used! But basically, for six months, you need to be one of the people who ...

- plans
- prepares
- prays
- presents stuff

... with children. All four aspects are important. Experience of all four will lay the foundation for this Unit – and for all the other Units as well.

By the end of such an experience, your knowledge of children and gut-level reaction to them will be quite different from how it was before. That's what you need if the material in this Unit is going to be very much help to you.

For your notes.....

The art of observation

If you want to understand children, you have to accustom your eyes to 'see' children in some detail, and to notice the behaviours which confirm the theories as well as those which are unusual. Maybe you are well used to doing this kind of observing or perhaps it is a new experience for you. Whichever is true for you, take time to watch the group of children you normally lead or are thinking of leading.

In a busy group it is not usually possible for one member of the leadership team to sit back and watch – but that is what I am suggesting you do. You will need to make arrangements with another leader, because while you are watching the group of children you will not be able to be responsible for them. You need to be free from any other tasks.

Sit at the side of the room, or watch through a window, or sit in on an activity which is fairly undemanding – a dough table is good because your hands can be occupied without you having to concentrate on what they are doing. If you find you have to be involved in an activity like this because it is too disconcerting for the children to have you there otherwise, go to your notebook regularly and scribble down comments and points you want to remember (even though you might think you will remember them afterwards...).

Here are some questions to help to focus your attention, but don't feel bound by them. You can photocopy these pages and use them time and again as observation sheets.

How big is the group of children?

How many carers or responsible adults are there?

Does the group have a buzz/feel busy/ look unsettled/seem lethargic?

Are there individual children who are spectators?

Is there one group of children which is 'in charge'?

Are some leaders more in demand than others?

Do the leaders give a sense of everything being under control? Are there moments when children are not sure what to do?

Is there one child who is more demanding than any other?

Can you see any child who is totally absorbed by their own activity and unaware of anyone else?

Is anyone bored and unattracted to any activity?

Is the room attractive – lighting, colours, layout, sense of welcome?

Are the leaders attractive – welcoming, good-natured, well prepared?

At the beginning, do children arrive with enthusiasm?

At the end, are they waiting around to go?

Knowing me, knowing you

O Lord you have searched me
and you know me.
You know when I sit and when I rise;
and you perceive my thoughts from afar.
You discern my going out and my lying down;
you are familiar with all my ways.
Before a word is on my tongue
you know it completely, O Lord.
You hem me in – behind and before;
you lay your hand upon me.
Such knowledge is too wonderful for me,
too lofty for me to attain.

Psalm 139:1-6

Knowledge of ourselves is a valuable commodity. Knowing ourselves, understanding how we think and act, recognising our weaknesses and enjoying our strengths – all of these are necessary keys to being able to understand other people.

A natural part of being human is to want to know others and to want to know ourselves. One of the endless delights of being with children is to allow them to get to know us and to realise that they are allowing us to know them too. This Unit is to help us to grow that knowledge.

There is space on these pages to introduce four children. Answer any questions, stick in the photo or sketch, and add any other information which you find relevant. Take time over this – enjoy thinking about each person in turn. If you are unable to answer some of the questions, particularly about temperament and home background, don't be tempted to pry or find out information in an unhelpful way. The four children should be:

- A child from your observation location (school, other church, etc)

- A child from your own group (or your church group if you're not yet a leader)

- Another child from your own group

- Yourself as a child!

Here is your first opportunity to take a photo or, if that's not possible in your situation, to draw a sketch or create a 'word sketch'. Remember to make sure that you have permission before taking photos.

Look out for this image to remind you.

Your photo or sketch from your observation visit

1. Name _____

age:

dark / fair

energetic / lethargic

talkative / quiet

creative / reticent

sporty / reflective

friendly / shy

only child / siblings

single parent / two parents / guardian

serious / playful

Your photo or sketch from your observation visit

2. Name _____

age:

dark / fair

energetic / lethargic

talkative / quiet

creative / reticent

sporty / reflective

friendly / shy

only child / siblings

single parent / two parents / guardian

serious / playful

Your photo or sketch from your observation visit

3. Name _____

age:

dark / fair

energetic / lethargic

talkative / quiet

creative / reticent

sporty / reflective

friendly / shy

only child / siblings

single parent / two parents / guardian

serious / playful

Your photo or sketch from your observation visit

4. Name _____

age:

dark / fair

energetic / lethargic

talkative / quiet

creative / reticent

sporty / reflective

friendly / shy

only child / siblings

single parent / two parents / guardian

serious / playful

In touch with your past?

Before you go on to think more about children today, spend some time thinking about your own childhood. Maybe you don't remember much about yourself as a child. Well, this is your opportunity to get to know yourself better by digging out some photos, asking relations some questions, and giving yourself time to remember!

You can make a few notes here – but try to insert extra pages as you discover more information.

The making of the child

Assemble four different colour highlighters, one for each of the four children you have introduced on the previous pages. As you read these pages about child development, pick out the statements which apply to each of your children.

Social development

Up until a child goes to school their social development is steadily leading them to growing independence from the parents and other carers. As this independence begins to emerge, the baby will first form relationships with other members of the family and close friends, while being timid with strangers or occasional visitors. Increasingly the toddler begins to take notice of the children they are playing side-by-side with and to communicate with other adults.

Throughout the pre-school and early school Foundation Stage there is a growing desire to be accepted by other people and to please them. There is a tendency to have favourite people who are looked up to with awe and quoted with great authority. Some would say social development is damaged or hindered by solitary activities such as TV and DVD, computer games, Playstation, and so on.

During the later years of primary school this desire to socialise and belong crystallises in an enjoyment of clubs. It will often find a focus in special friendships with people who have been picked out of the group.

> Where can I go from your Spirit?
> Where can I flee from your presence?
> If I go up to the heavens, you are there;
> if I make my bed in the depths, you are there.
> If I rise on the wings of the dawn,
> if I settle on the far side of the sea,
> even there your hand will guide me,
> your right hand will hold me fast.
>
> Psalm 139:7-10

Physical development

From birth to playgroup the child grows rapidly. Every time a friend or neighbour sees the baby or toddler, the growth and development of skills is obvious – they can hold things, sit up, crawl or pull themselves up on furniture, then walk.

As their social life increases they learn to exercise greater control over their hands and feet. They also begin to communicate clearly not only with an increased vocabulary but with gestures and eye contact. There is some evidence that even at this early stage boys will develop a little slower than girls. Issues such as potty-training will be a challenge for both parents and children, and boys are likely to be slower.

Before they go to school they can often use basic sport skills of catching and throwing, climbing and running, jumping and skipping. All these skills continue to improve as they go through school, with a sense of competition exercising a strong incentive to improve co-ordination and 'to win'! It is at this stage that physical ailments move through schools in phases, and milk teeth are slowly and painfully replaced. As the physical growth pattern slows down, the body has the chance to enhance its fitness with finer co-ordination, although spurts of restless energy often spoil this.

> For you created my inmost being;
> you knit me together in my mother's womb.
> I praise you because I am fearfully and wonderfully made;
> your works are wonderful, I know that full well.
> My frame was not hidden from you
> when I was made in the secret place.
> When I was woven together in the depths of the earth,
> your eyes saw my unformed body.
> All the days ordained for me were written in your book
> before one of them came to be.
>
> Psalm 139:13-16

Intellectual development

From the moment the baby realises that there is a difference between other objects or people and themselves, their intellectual development can be observed easily. The baby and toddler will imitate both people and toys. To begin with their pleasure is in taking control of a toy but later as language grows they will want to know the reasons why something is happening as it is. Many parents and carers will be frustrated by the constant question 'Why?'

There is always a smudged line in their imagination between fact and fiction so they are at their most secure with concrete thinking and examples.

As they go into playgroup and school so the ability to order and classify, to separate into groups and to add the groups together grows. Maths is often done with triumph, and facts are not only picked up quickly but passed on with pleasure.

As the later years of primary education approach so the distinction between the world of fact and the world of the imagination becomes clearer and reasoning becomes more concrete and logical. This means that proof, or reasons why, will be required of any arguments from someone else.

> How precious to me are your thoughts, O God!
> How vast is the sum of them!
> Were I to count them, they would outnumber the grains of sand.
> When I awake, I am still with you.
> Psalm 139:17-18

Moral development

Before playgroup age there is no sense of right or wrong in a baby or toddler – the criteria used is, 'Is it enjoyable?' But slowly the sense grows that life is pleasanter when parents are pleased – perhaps there is a natural desire there to please people too.

By the time school is reached, rewards and punishments steer behaviour powerfully, but a dilemma arises as peer group and authority figures produce agonising alternatives. The child usually tries to obey the rules of the group. This is also when a strong sense of justice grows, and the argument against blame and guilt is, 'It isn't fair!'

> If only you would slay the wicked, O God!
> Away from me you bloodthirsty men!
> They speak of you with evil intent;
> your adversaries misuse your name.
> Do I not hate those who rise up against you?
> I have nothing but hatred for them;
> I count them my enemies.
>
> Search me, O God, and know my heart;
> test me and know my anxious thoughts.
> See if there is any offensive way in me,
> and lead me in the way everlasting.
> Psalm 139:19-24

Handling disability

It is easy to pick out patterns of development in babies, toddlers and children. The patterns are not uniform and it is not unusual to find wide variation, but any extreme variation from the norm should be checked medically. When this is detected in early babyhood or in the first days at school, this can raise anxieties, but often the condition will right itself in a healthy child and the anxiety will prove unnecessary.

However there are children who are damaged when they are born and others who show early signs of disability. We should also be aware that some forms of autism do not become apparent until a child is 2 or 3. The awareness that a child has a disability sometimes causes lifelong challenges for the child themselves and sadness and struggles for their carers.

The church has traditionally ignored disability. In biblical days anything which was not the norm was regarded as a mark of the evil one. This attitude was taken up in medieval times and often still persists today. People, including Christians, are embarrassed by disability, and are irritated by the different environment it demands. Within easy reach of most churches there are schools or residential centres for children with disability. Yet many churches have none in their children's groups in church. These are children who are cut off from the social activities of life and avidly want to make connections with normal events in society – like the church community. Why don't they feel welcome?

As you sketch out the development patterns of your four children, you may well find that they all fit into what we consider a 'normal pattern'. Does that mean that your local school and church are not welcoming disability? Is this an issue you have ever considered? Is there room for your church to develop in this area of work?

> If I say, "Surely the darkness will hide me
> and the light become night around me,"
> even darkness will not be dark to you;
> the night will shine like the day,
> for darkness is as light to you.
>
> Psalm 139:11-12

Notes

Assignment 2

If you are studying this course with a tutor you should have already completed Assignment 1, which is the Starter Essay that enables you to introduce yourself to your tutor. Now do the second assignment.

My own church

Write a letter to your church leadership/PCC/elders explaining how you would like to see children's work develop in your church over the next five years. Maximum 800 words. Send one copy to your Tutor for marking, and give the other to your church leadership. Use this page and the next for your first draft.

How faith grows

This Unit considers how the human development of a child, and the development of a trusting faith in God, relate to each other and interact. You consider how you can help this process.

Contents

Watching faith grow

This Unit will assume a certain amount of knowledge and understanding about how faith develops and grows in people. If you don't have that already, you need to set about getting it before launching into this Unit.

Depending on your Christian background, you are likely to respond to theories of faith development in children in different ways, and see different ways of applying the theories to church practice:

- Some people will look to an official church pattern of child nurture designed to prepare them for their first communion, confirmation, baptism, or other mark of Christian belonging.

- Some will want to teach the Bible systematically to their children, and will see the way that each child responds to that teaching as a spiritual issue and nothing to do with psychology.

- Some would see the marks of spiritual life in a child as being the same as those in an adult.

Most of us would see belief in an unseen world as vital to faith – followed by the ability to make connections between what we can see and what we cannot see. The Faith Development Theories look at the stages of a person's growing ability to do this.

Your reactions to the theories of faith development will have been formed in the framework of:

- seeing faith grow in the children in your church or other group

- seeing faith grow in your own life

Before you start this Unit you need to be aware of both.

Start by reading

You might like to prepare by reading a book about the work of researchers Fowler and/or Westerhoff. You will need a basic understanding of the work of faith development theorists. The most accessible book is *Children Finding Faith*.

The point of doing this reading is to give you an opportunity to put the basic ideas of faith development into the context of the children you know. Stop in your reading as often as possible to ask the question, 'How does this relate to the children I already work with?'

Remember too that these are theories – and that many of the people who researched and came to these conclusions revised them later in life in the light of further experience or research evidence. The theories are not straightjackets into which we can put children. But they throw light on human life so that we can see some patterns and work with those patterns rather than against them.

J Astley (ed), *How Faith Grows: Faith Development and Christian Education*, National Society/Church House Publishing, 1994, Ch 1

J Astley & L J Francis (eds), *Christian Perspectives on Faith Development*, Gracewing /Fowler Wright, 1992, ISBN 0852442203

Frances Bridger, *Children Finding Faith*, SU, 2003

James Fowler, *Stages of Faith*, HarperSanFrancisco, 1995

J Westerhoff, *Will Our Children Have Faith?*, Crossroad/Seabury Press, 1976

Start by drawing

Take a long strip of wall paper – say about 2m long (if you're over 50, that's about 6 ft...). Use a thick felt-tip and draw out the journey of your own faith so far.

Start by drawing along the piece of paper the main events of your childhood. This is not an entrance for an art competition, so just draw simply the things which come to mind as you think back – the people who were family when you were born, a house for when you moved home, or the railings for the day you started school, a tent for the earliest holiday memory, and so on.

Now go back through it again. What were your ideas about God at different points in your life and how have they changed? Again this is not a theology exam, so write things down simply – and truthfully. This will take time. It will also be more fun if you do the remembering alongside a friend. Mark your journey with a cross at any point where you have a specific memory about spiritual things.

Knowledge about Faith Development Theories will not solve all your problems but it will underpin the work you do with children. And it will give you a deeper understanding of that process of faith development which should be going on in us as leaders all the time.

For your notes:

The growth of trust

The Faith Development Theories of our century have tried to define the stages through which the majority of people of all ages travel. Psychologists have hazarded a guess as to the speed and likely obstacles in the pathway through those stages.

Such insights can help the pastor and the evangelist to plan their approach to children within the community of faith. It gives children's leaders realistic hopes for what the responses and reactions might be to their approach.

Learning to pray

It is exciting to see a child's faith in God develop. But what counts as 'faith development' is wide and varied. Prayer is a good example.

Children learn patterns of prayer from the people they spend time with at home, in church and at school. They may learn to pray with a grandparent or godparent. They may draw on examples which they are able to explore in private as individuals, and on ones which use the corporate expression of the congregation.

As the child experiences prayer in terms of both talking and listening, as they begin to understand something of God's response to prayer, a maturity grows which often outstrips the adult. We may try to protect God from having to 'answer prayers' in case the child is disappointed. We may find ourselves anxiously trying to help the child with the silence involved in listening – but actually neither of these may be any problem to a child whose relationship with God is growing and developing. Instead we may find our own lives of prayer looking a little vulnerable and empty compared with the trust and confidence found in the child. If nothing else, working with children can help us think through our own prayer lives.

Learning to worship

We may find ourselves preparing children for participation in a communion service. We struggle to explain the inexplicable, but if we pause and listen to the child we often find that the child has gone before us. There are images and steps of faith which have already been made and leave us as followers and not leaders.

Or we may see spiritual development in the ability to sustain an interest in corporate worship or to enjoy the sophisticated meaning in the words of a hymn.

Such things may feel strange, and as a leader or a parent you may feel insecure – after all, adults are used to being the ones to walk ahead. But, whatever age we are, God works in our lives unseen, teaching us things we have no memory of ever learning.

Learning to speak

Then there is the spiritual phenomenon of a child who is given for one occasion a spiritual gift to use in the company of God's people – suddenly speaking out of a deep knowledge of God's presence, sensing the voice of his Holy Spirit and producing profound spiritual wisdom in a situation.

Adults, feeling an instinctive need to explain such a precocious contribution, may find themselves saying, 'Out of the mouths of babes' and laughing, or 'He doesn't understand what he's saying' – and ignoring the appropriate quality of what has been said. Far better to take what has been said seriously and acknowledge evidence of something splendid and profound – something which should produce awe and celebration in all of us.

For your notes:

Signs to look for

As we work with children in our care, we can be observant about what is going on in their lives with God. That will help us work with them in a way appropriate to their 'stage' of faith.

Here are some things to look for:

We are different

You may notice that a child is able to distinguish the difference between their own feelings and those of another person. They show some recognition that they are different from other people, not only in their life-style and family rules but also in what they think and how they react – their opinions. This is important for the way we relate in our pluralistic world. It is also important for how we respond to God – who says that His thoughts are not our thoughts, neither are His ways our ways.

But is it right?

You may see that the attitude of the child is changing in terms of seeing things as right or wrong – rather than simply looking to see the reaction of the adults and gauging the incident by their reactions. Many children will feel strongly about injustice and may be very vocal and indignant if they see you or others in authority not behaving in a just manner.

Who I belong to

Another pointer to developing faith is the way in which a child's attitude about belonging changes and grows. At the early stages we are likely to limit the people who belong to us as being very intimate and immediate, whereas several stages of faith later we may be able to grasp a sense of belonging to everything which breathes.

Who to listen to

We also grow in how we see authority and who we recognise it in. We rely on authority for the shape of our lives and the sense of rightness and even achievement in it. A young child takes authority from those adults most closely involved in their life. In later stages we change and realign ourselves with other authority sources – the peer group, the government, the church or a cult figure. Many of us move into positions of authority, and exercise that power wisely or badly!

How we see the world

This is linked strongly with our world view. World view is something we are at first 'dressed in' by those who take responsibility for us. Later on, we take responsibility for it ourselves and our world view belongs to us. As that happens, we develop the confidence to experience others with a different world faith from us and still to feel accepted – even to enjoy the difference!

> *All these marks grow as each stage of faith development is travelled and new growth is welcomed.*

In marking out the stages of faith development, it is important to emphasise the word 'theory'. As psychologists have continued to explore and puzzle over the results of their research, so they have adjusted (and in some cases, radically rethought) their findings. So long as we recognise the setting for these theories, we will be able to find them revealing and helpful. If we 'set them in stone' or use them as prescribed patterns to lay ahead of a child, we will be doing the child and the church a great disservice.

Friends

I fear it's very wrong of me
     And yet I must admit
When someone offers friendship
     I want the whole of it.
I don't want everybody else
     To share my friends with me.
At least I want one special one,
     Who indisputably,
Likes me much much more than all the rest
     Who's always on my side,
Who never cares what others say,
     Who lets me come and hide
Within his shadow, in his house –
     It doesn't matter where –
Who lets me simply be myself,
     Who's always, always there.

       (Elizabeth Jennings, 'All in a day')

A display of faith

Collect together any poems, stories or pictures which children have made about their faith and their relationship with God. Spend time enjoying them, either with them or on your own. With their permission, make a display of them for the whole church to enjoy, in a place where people have plenty of privacy and space to read them.

You can make some notes here but you will probably need to add extra pages to display what you have collected.

Remember the children you thought of on pages 25 and 26. Keep them in your mind as you read the following pages. Make connections between what you know about them and what you read in the text. They will not fit exactly – no-one does!

Stages of faith

Feet and faith

There is a natural way for feet to develop and grow. If the right shoes provide space for the growth, the feet will be healthy; but if not the child will be crippled and lame.

In the same way, faith development will naturally occur, but what we provide in terms of space and encouragement can help ensure that the growth is healthy and strong.

In marking out the stages of faith development it is helpful to identify with the work of one psychologist. We will take the work of James Fowler as our example. His work is held in high regard on the grounds both of the level of research he conducted and his own professional handling of the results.

Fowler claims that there are six stages of faith and that these are universal – although not many people pursue the developmental pattern through to the end. These stages are not dramatic or sudden changes from one band of growth to the next, but gradual changes with periods of transition.

The transitions can be triggered by crisis or challenge, when something unexpected shakes the pattern of our life. When this happens, we are 'pulled loose' and some new expression of faith draws us. We move on, our faith being restructured as we go, continually reviewing our knowledge and impression of God.

A question of process

The study of faith development is a study of the processes of faith rather than the content of faith. This process is seen as common to all people – part of being human – rather than something through which only religious people progress.

At the time we don't notice the stage we are travelling through, and can't define it as this or that. But looking back we can often identify some of the stages of faith the researchers define. As we hear a stage described, we know we have been there, and travelled that way.

Fowler identified the need for prolonged and in depth conversations before this research could be completed. We are rarely able to pursue conversations at such depth with the children in our groups. But our familiarity with this research will help us to see signs of their journey – and through noticing that, we can see the signs of where we are too!

Stage 0: Foundation Faith
0-4 years

Obviously the early years of this stage are purely observation – no child of one year old speaks with lucidity about their faith. At this stage Fowler sees the child receiving its identity from its mother in an environment which is defined by faces, breasts and hands. As the child learns to recognise smiles and holds the contact of eyes so there is the first stage of a life-long faith, learning to trust and to be nurtured.

Stage 1: Unordered Faith
3/4 - 6/7 years

The mind and imagination of a child of this age is bombarded with different images, and the distinction between those which are imagined and those which are real is unclear. There are some boundaries which keep the child from becoming lost in such a world, but any new story or information tends to be simply added to this mixture and construed on the level of everything else. The impact of the story or information on the child is in proportion to the person providing it – the big adult is a seriously important person.

At this stage of faith the child imitates those who are around – especially the important adults. That's why the quality of parenting at this stage is a crucial aspect of life, providing dependable images and role models.

At this stage 'God is like…' is more likely to be 'fire' or 'wind' than a 'Big brother watching you' or 'Grandfather'.

Stage 2: Ordering Faith
6/7 - 11/12 years

The child is now developing a real ability to think and sort, to follow through patterns and logic. They feel more in control of their world and want to know the difference between fact and fiction in what they are being told.

Narrative is powerful. But in the child's mind there is now a difference between a story on a video and the world in which they live. They can retell the story of the video and not muddle it up with their own world. They can see themselves as separate from the story, but also choose to be part of it and insert themselves into it.

The child will be keen to join and belong, will take on the rules and faith of the group, and will be overt in expressing their commitment to the group and its believing.

The images of God will be more likely to be that of judge and king – the omnipotent controller.

Some adults are still at this stage. There is no law which forces people to move on to the next stage.

Stage 3: Conforming Faith
11/12 - 17/18 years and adult

At this stage there is a new self-awareness and a reflective ability – which leads to a new way of relating and new kinds of relationships. I want to conform to the significant people around me – the adults who still form the safe structure of my life. These are the people I have chosen to have authority over me; I want to please them and be accepted by them. By accepting their authority, their beliefs and values are therefore mine. I go with the flow of faith around me and live to these moral standards.

Although this is an exciting stage of faith to be involved with, it is also very complicated. Any evangelism which sets up a challenge to the beliefs of the adults round the young person, will be setting that young person in a dilemma.

In terms of faith development this can be very fruitful – triggering the developing person into a new stage – but it is also very painful. The young person tries to juggle with all the people around them who are making demands or setting standards – parents, teachers, leaders, sports coach, peer group. They find themselves asking questions about their identity which they have never had to ask before. They are faced with the question, 'Who am I?'

Stage 4: Choosing Faith
17/18 years - 30s/40s

This stage screams for personal uniqueness. It is no longer enough for me to be a reflection of someone else, or for my faith to be an extension of theirs. This is my faith and part of my unique being.

Instead of my faith being a blanket within which caring people have kept me cocooned, it is now something I can stand back from and consider. The tendency now is to make it tidy and neat, to get rid of any messiness about it, to so order it that it all fits neatly together. That is often the way people who are new converts to a faith talk and act – they have the thing neatly tied up and every problem ironed out (in a way we haven't after years of journeying!).

This is an important stage of faith, and one where a person needs plenty of support, encouragement and good personal relationships.

Stage 5: Balanced Faith

7% of Fowler's research sample go on to a further stage. Often this is as a result of trauma, failure and disappointment. The neatness of Stage 4 disappears. As faith seems to fall apart at the seams, it is reworked and rethought at a different level – in the light of the pain and difficulty.

This reworking and recognition of difficulties in the life of faith makes us more open to the opinions and stances of other people. This in turn has an impact on our view of serving others, as well as on how we view faith. There is a balanced approach to faith which holds different perspectives in tension and does not seek easy or trite answers.

Stage 6: Selfless Faith

People at this stage are likely to go out to change the world, even if they die in the attempt. They recognise their place in the world community, and they carry with them the big picture, a wide vision and set of values. There is a deep commitment to find truth and to live it out among others who are to be served – without there ever being the need to arrive and find it!

Notes

Lines on a clock in Chester Cathedral

When I was a child, I laughed and wept,

Time crept.

When I was a youth, I dreamt and talked,

Time walked.

When I became a full-grown man,

Time ran.

When older still I daily grew,

Time flew.

Soon I shall find on travelling on –

Time gone.

O Christ, wilt Thou have saved me then?

Amen.

(Henry Twells)

One step closer

The theories are just a light shining on the complicated puzzle of faith development, rather than a straightjacket to fit people into. So it is worth looking at the work of another psychologist. Engel identified a series of steps of faith which has come to be called 'The Engel Scale' They are not steps attached to particular ages or to stages of life. Obviously not all the steps get to be completed by everyone. The steps are:

- aware of the supernatural
- aware of Christianity
- interest in Christianity
- aware of the basic facts of the gospel
- grasp of the implications of the gospel
- positive attitude to the gospel
- aware of personal need
- challenge and decision to act
- repentance and faith
- commitment

The interesting thing is to look at the implications the steps have for different generations. For example, in my parents' generation, most children were at step four when they went to school. They were aware of the basic facts of the gospel whether they came from a churched family or not. Today children are often ignorant of those facts even when they are members of a church.

A questionnaire in a school where there was a cross-section of cultures showed that in a class of bright 10 year olds the children whose parents were members of local Christian churches knew very little more facts of the gospel than those from other faiths. But all of those children were aware of the supernatural – step one – and a lot of their play and creative writing was around themes of supernatural power and mystery.

John Finney is one of the people who has led our thinking about evangelism during the last decades. He has suggested a diagram (adapted below) for describing not so much the journey of faith as the starting point of faith – the way in which people consciously become aware of a growing commitment to the Christian life. He thinks of entry points as doorways which have a corresponding doorway on the axis across the circle. (From *Church on the Move*, Daybreak 1992, page 152)

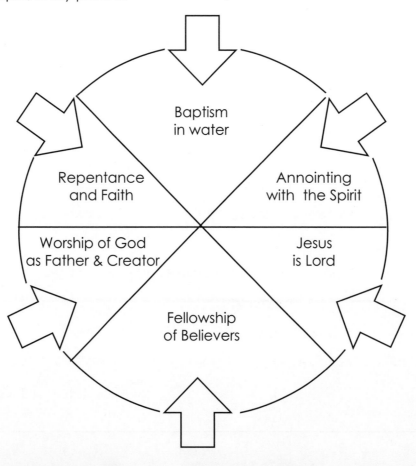

Baptism in water

Repentance and Faith

Annointing with the Spirit

Worship of God as Father & Creator

Jesus is Lord

Fellowship of Believers

Catholic axis

There is an axis which goes across from the Baptism in Water to Fellowship of Believers – this axis emphasises the corporate nature of the faith. This is the catholic entry point which would seem to some to be too mechanical.

Evangelical axis

Then there is the axis of the evangelical with the two entry points of Repentance and Faith and Jesus is Lord. This gives an emphasis on the personal response to the love of God in Christ, and would seem to some people to be too individualistic.

Pentecostal axis

Finally there is the axis which offers the two entry points of the Anointing with the Spirit and Worship of God the Father axis which concentrates on a direct experience of God through the Holy Spirit. This approach would be seen by some as too experiential.

For each of these sets of doorways, ask yourself:

- How would primary age children react and respond to this doorway?
- What would be their likely introduction to the faith?
- What response would seem to be appropriate to the adults involved?
- What would their image be of the church and their place in it?

Write some notes in the boxes.

Catholic/corporate

Evangelical/personal

Pentecostal/experiential

In fact, each needs to learn from the other two in order to appreciate the richness of the Christian Faith. All are possible ways for a person to come to faith in God through Jesus Christ, but none on its own will draw all the children in your care to their own faith in a God who loves them.

Space for your own notes....

The journey

One way of describing the process of entering, and growing, in faith is to picture the life of faith as a pilgrimage. Everyone is travelling together along the road of life – through a variety of countryside, perhaps symbolising the experience of each other's company. The picture is a good one.

- It illustrates how people are at different points along the road but can be going together in the same direction.
- It gives us a sense of purpose and final destiny, as well as the value of the present part of our journey.
- It makes each stage of the journey valid in itself – the fact that each stage of the journey is vital and unmissable becomes obvious.
- It makes the journey last from the cradle to the grave, and this sustained approach to faith – our own and that of the children in our care – will save us from looking for fast-result evangelism.

As with all faith theories or metaphors, this model offers some helpful ideas but still leaves some questions.

How many different ways of joining the road can you identify?

..... they might be born to a pilgrim mother

......

......

......

How many different ways can you think that pilgrims might have to choose to stay on the road or be confused about which way to go?

..... they might cross another road with other pilgrims on it

......

......

......

Once they have started to travel, how confident will they be of the way they are going and how sure of their destination?

.....

.....

.....

What will sustain and strengthen them from day to day? And from night to night?

.....

.....

.....

How well will they relate to the different pilgrims on the road? Will they always travel with the same people? What might affect this?

.....

.....

.....

Assignment 3

If you are studying this course with a tutor you must do this assignment.

Focused in words

Focus your learning so far by writing one of the following assignments. Try to write about 800-1000 words.

1 How does the teaching plan or programme you have followed in your children's group during the last year take the theories of faith development seriously?

2 How do you relate the idea of a faith journey to your own experience of Christianity? How might this affect how you relate to children?

Send the completed assignment to your tutor for marking by post or email.

A culture of their own

This Unit expands the basic features of the culture of the young today.
It helps us as adults see across a cultural gap that is just as wide as that between whole societies in the world.

Contents

The media culture

Children and adults today belong to two different worlds, and there are many things that influence the young. Keeping in touch with culture is one of the greatest challenges for any adult, and especially teachers or leaders of children. The way an adult sees the world is quite different from the way a child sees it.

Traditionally the church has required a child to sit still, listen to an adult's perspective, and learn to think as an adult. When the child can speak the language of the adults, we 'test' their understanding, and on the basis of the 'right' answers given in the right language we have allowed them to become members of God's church.

It would always have been better to go about working with children the other way round. The first requirement for adults who want to become leaders or teachers of children should be that they listen to children and learn how to think as a child. That makes a lot more sense in terms of communication – and it has a good basis in the teaching of Jesus.

In this Unit we are aiming to get inside the world of the child. For any adult who wants to work with children, it is important to understand what it is like to be a child in today's world. You will never be that child, of course. We cannot leave behind the experience and maturity which has made us the adults that we are. But we can make some efforts to get inside this modern young world – by looking at those things which influence them. In particular we need to look at the values which are strongly communicated through the media (TV, video and DVD, internet) and through printed resources (magazines and books).

Here are a few facts and figures to get you thinking:

- On average children watch over 3 hours of live TV per day, plus DVD and internet viewing
- 'Eastenders' (BBC soap serial) is the most popular TV programme with 8-11 year olds
- Up to half of all children watch TV after 9pm unsupervised

You may feel that you have good contact with what children watch on TV already. If the television is on in the corner of the room while you get the children their tea, you may feel you are in touch with what they are watching. But that programme is not getting the attention you need to give it if you are to assess and analyse it.

There are three pieces of experiential preparation to do before launching into this Unit. Even the most experienced of us can benefit from this sort of preparation, because the world of the child changes so rapidly.

Write down, at least in note form, a description of the values and assumptions which are conveyed in all these forms of children's entertainment. Better still, discuss each with a friend who will do the preparation with you. If there are others doing this course with you, discuss it with them. Otherwise you will probably notice what you expect to be there, rather than come to terms with things that will change the way you think.

In this process you may find yourself remembering the equivalent experience in your own childhood. If you do, make sure you are honest about it! It is easy to be negative and be full of the 'good old days'. When you find things which are of concern, look for other things which make you feel pleased for young people today – because both are there.

Notes

TV

Plan to view and review six hours of children's and 'family' television programmes over a 7-10 day period. Choose a variety of types of programme, and select programmes aimed at each end of the age-range you are preparing to lead. Remember that any programme broadcast before 9pm is considered to be suitable for family viewing, and that soaps are very popular with children.

Up to a third of all children watch TV after 9pm unsupervised

Magazines

Purchase a range of children's comic and magazines, and some for teenagers too. Remember that younger children read teenage magazines.

First, skim read and look at the design, colours and images to get a feel of the impact of it – the impact which is intended to make someone buy it. The producers of this magazine have done their market research – they know children and young people really well. They know how to market a magazine and sell it to that age-group (or to the parent if it's for the youngest age-group). Then read the magazine through from cover to cover a couple of times. As you read, ask yourself, 'What message is being given here about school, or home, or image, or buying things, or spirituality?'

Books

Choose six books which are currently popular with children. Don't just choose six yourself, because you will choose the ones you enjoyed when you were a child! The magazines you buy may suggest some, a bookshop or librarian may suggest what are the 'best sellers', or ask a few children what they are into. Again, choose books which represent the range within your chosen age-group. Then read them!

Films and Internet

Some children's films have a traditional feel about them, and often work on two levels so that both children and adults can enjoy them together. Children see them through their own cultural filter, and in due course the preparation process suggested here will help you to do that too.

Find out what videos/DVDs have been seen at recent birthday parties and get hold of those, or ask children about films they've seen. Watch a few of them, looking at the messages that are evident in the design, plot and presentation.

Talk to some children about how they use the internet, and ask them to show you what they watch. Talk to them about social networking sites (Bebo, Facebook) and at shared video sites such as YouTube. Consider the advantages and risks of this medium.

Eastenders (BBC soap serial) is the most popular TV programme with 8-11 year olds

Notes

A culture of variety

There are six basic assumptions which underpin our culture today.

We are in charge of our own destiny. Any problem is seen as having a solution – whether that problem is a disease or any other scientific challenge. You just need to invest the right amount of money into the thinking time needed to sort it out. Where a former generation might have believed in God – or blamed God – for the mess or delight of what was happening around them in society, people of our time trust in themselves. They can think through anything and understand it.

We believe in progress. The world we are creating around ourselves is improving all the time (we are told). The combination of science and technology give people the opportunity for an improved lifestyle and a better standard of living.

We value objectivity. We expect to be asked to believe what we can see with our own eyes to be true – what we can work out for ourselves and for which we can understand the proof.

It is everyone's right to believe what they want. That is the ultimate freedom which humanity has been striving for in recent generations.

Religion is a matter of private opinion. Faith is different from facts – facts can be proved and faith cannot. So it's up to each person to decide what they will believe, since none of it can be proved anyway.

Everyone is basically good. The church is simply wrong about original sin, and about an inherent inclination in humanity to do wrong.

Isn't there a discrepancy between what we have always seen as quality of life and what we are experiencing in our society today?

- Many people in modern society are feeling hopeless, caught in a cycle of debt, addiction or bad relationships.

- Despair is a common emotion – the sense that there will never be anything better and that no-one cares.

- We have failed to answer the challenge of the destruction of the ozone layer or the rain forest, the possibility of nuclear destruction, the problem of AIDS.

- We have been working for tolerance and freedom for everyone on the planet but become more and more suspicious of each other.

- We have lost the skill of sustaining life together, and operate within a selfish world-view.

The New Age Movement and other 'open' spirituality, with its mixture of worshipping the Mother Earth and its options for spirit guides and re-incarnation, has a strong following and is influencing the way spiritual experience is encouraged in schools. The Movement reflects the spiritual hunger of our time, gives people spiritual experience, offers hope (especially for the planet), and encourages community. In listening to these sentiments, children will be hearing some Christian phrases and images, but ultimately they will not hear a Christian message. There will be no advocacy for a need to turn to God for forgiveness, or for a need for repentance to enable godly living.

This style of spirituality is a mixture of aspects of many faiths, and can give a false sense of familiarity with these religions. It is characteristic of a society where there are many faiths on offer – especially to children. The religious variety experienced by children in school as part of the National Curriculum can be confusing and overwhelming. It is like a supermarket of faith in which (it is argued) the only sensible approach is to keep our options open and our minds unmade!

Schoolchildren with a strong Christian faith may find themselves accused of having entrenched views and untaught opinions. Our children day-by-day go into an arena of religious discussion which would stretch an adult's faith and debating skills to the full. The new possibilities of religious faith leave none unchallenged.

Read

Collect two or three newspapers for one day. Look at the content of the news and the way in which it is communicated.

What do you think the main message of each paper is?

Is it optimistic or pessimistic?

Is its emphasis on fact or narrative?

Is the narrative aimed at action to improve the world?

Will the way in which it is written cause people to be entertained by news – or depressed by it?

Rewrite...

Rewrite one of the main items of news – maybe one which has appeared in all the papers in your set. Write the news episode in order to give the facts clearly and concisely. Make sure that what you encourage in the reader is hope for change. Make any community action which is feasible accessible to them.

If this was your church newspaper...

What comment from the church would you want to give?

What passage from the Bible would be appropriate to use to comment, to warn, to encourage or to instruct?

A culture of

Descartes summed up his philosophy of life with the Latin words

"Cogito, ergo sum" – "I think, therefore I am"

What makes us uniquely human, uniquely valuable, is that we think, we reflect, we are aware.

The phrase for our present generation might well be 'Tesco, ergo sum' – I shop, therefore I am. This is a prominent feature of the post-modern world; we place considerable emphasis on our belongings. And the emphasis falls not on the great inherited wealth from our history, but on the enticing, affordable, ever-changing fashions and fads of the high street shops. We gain identity no longer from how we earn our money ('What shall I be when I grow up'?), but from how we spend it ('Do I wear Nike, Adidas or Ellesse?').

Children have long been the targets of the marketing people, who recognize that in today's culture children have access to more money than anyone else. Long before children have access to independent funds, they are at the mercy of commercial advertising. Television, their main source of entertainment, continually bombards them between programmes with enticing sales-talk, attractive images and desirable goods, and advertising is strong on the internet. Advertisers know that when one child has something, other children want it – and their parents want the kudos gained by their child having what that other child has or easily give in to the phenomenal strength of 'pester power'. And so it goes on.

Like adults?

Many of the objects which are marketed with children in mind are small versions of an adult parallel. Clothes for children are no longer children's clothes – they are small adults' fashion. Children are entered for beauty pageants before they start school, and learn to do make-up in nursery. It is not simply the product which is a reflection of the adult world – it is also the technique for selling it. There are strong sexual images used to market goods to children even of an early age. This is one of the reasons why children are much more informed about sexual practice, because it is the coinage used to catch their attention in the market place.

Real desires?

Some of the toys which are recent hits on the scene have no parallel nor any counterpart in real life at all – like mechanical toys which can be changed from one form into another, or marketing tie-ins with TV programmes or films. The child can have had no prior longing to possess such an object since they are totally imaginary. Such toys depend completely on marketing not only for being sold but for giving them a reason for existing in the first place. These toys are often expensive (not pocket money level), and their themes are carried across to other products. The result is the creation of a cult where to own is to belong.

Another desire is the desire for instant fame, stardom and riches. Children are exposed in every way to 'reality TV' and talent shows where people become instantly famous and get everything they have ever wanted. Likewise YouTube videos can get thousands of views, and create 'stars' almost instantly. This desire for stardom and fame goes beyond the daydream and into the heart and mind of children – they really believe that they will be the next great footballer, dancer or singer. Many teachers have seen this change and are becoming increasingly worried about the dangers of depression and despair when 99.9% realize that they will never get there.

marketing

Buying an identity?

In every age, playgrounds have wielded their influence, and the craze of the moment is the one to join. But there has never been a time when so much is available so readily to so many children. The money offered on credit to many parents is almost unlimited, and the shops offer a stunning range of goods from which to choose. Parenting skills have given way so much that in many homes children demand and get whatever they want, and as a result become increasingly demanding.

The emphasis for today's child is on owning and collecting. It doesn't matter if in a few week's time the article is dated and obsolete. Today it defines prestige and identity – both important issues in our society.

A growing concern is the contradiction of the numbers of children who are obese set against the increasing number of children with eating disorders. In a society that does everything 'to the max' we seem to be creating a world where children are thrown huge amounts of temptations, and yet are developing adult ideas about appearance, image, and 'thinness'.

Just having fun?

Much of the marketing of products is focused through the world of entertainment. It is there that we are relaxed and at our most vulnerable. At the cinema, watching a video or DVD, using the Internet – all these offer many opportunities to those who wish to advertise and collect customers.

Entertainment for children has been a rapidly changing scene for the last 25 years. With the arrival of video, personal computers and the Internet, children gained access to a large range of materials. Much of it can be used without adult permission or knowledge, and it does not rely on parental finance or time commitment for its availability. Maybe it is the first time that the recreation time of a child has moved outside the caring or permission zone of adults.

Gender issues

Boys are different from girls! OK, so this is no great surprise, but the differences are enhanced by the culture in which children live. Toys for boys are likely to be linked with cars, wars and aggression. Magazines and comics are in primary colours. Boys are pressurised to behave in a certain way, and girls are expected to be 'girly'. While society is perhaps too good at meeting the innate and often crude needs of boys, the church is very poor at it. Somewhere between the two is a good and stable balance. (See Nick Harding, *Boys, God and the Church*, Grove Booklet, 2007)

Judge by experience

Look back through the children's magazines you have been reading and think about the children's TV programmes you have been watching.

What were the main themes of the advertising?

If you introduce the person of Christ into that scene, what are the themes which are most shocking and repulsive, and which ones retain their attraction?

Then read through Ephesians 4:17 - 5:20 and think through some of the ways in which that could be interpreted in the world of children today.

Do some research

Ask some children about what they are buying and why.

What they would most like to get next?

What is their newest toy, game or item of clothing – and why did they want it?

Ask a local venue which is used for children's entertainment/sport, what sort of budget is used in order to attract children to it. Also, look at the different images which are used in their marketing. Does this tie up with anything the children told you?

Safety and childhood

Reflect on your time as a child. It is likely that you were allowed far more personal freedom to go out and play than many children are given today.

We live in a world where we have learned to mistrust others, and therefore fear that our children will be in danger if left to their own devices for a while. How does this affect how children see the world now?

Don't be like them

Children and young people don't want their parents to be like them – in fact when adults ape the young it causes real confusion. But they need the support of adults. They need adults who can say, "It's different now; tell us how it is! This is how it seems to us and this is our advice or reaction to your situation, but everything has changed so fast. We are right with you. You could try this, and if it doesn't turn out right, we'll be here on your side with unconditional love and commitment."

A culture of
individuals

The easiest way to cope with having a child around is to put the child in front of something which will grip their imagination. That child is then unlikely to make any demands on you.

That kind of child-minding is common practice today, in the home and elsewhere, often using videos or computer software which has not been vetted by the carer first. Children are at risk in our society through the world of entertainment, because adults have abdicated their responsibilities. Some of this may seem imposed on adults by the situation – the world of computer technology is not easy for adults to monitor, because they are not as able as their children in using it! But we have allowed entertainment to exploit our children in a way which should never have happened.

The fracturing of family

One of the reasons for this is that the pattern of our relationships has changed. Our expectations of friendships and family networks are now very different from what they were – both in terms of what we expect to receive and in what we expect to give.

- The 1950s brought the arrival of the motor car to the proud ownership of ordinary families. As a result, the world of each family member widened, and the network of relationships between them loosened. This continued with each new motorway built.

- The changes in employment patterns during recent years have widened the boundaries for many people about where they will work and live.

- Elderly parents live at one end of the country and their adult offspring at the other. Many young adults have not lived at home since they left for college or university.

- With over half of marriages ending in divorce, and most of those break-ups involving children, for many the nuclear family simply does not exist, or changes frequently.

- Some grandchildren meet their grandparents perhaps once or twice a year on an official visit.

- Young parents live out with their own children the detached relationship they have had with their own parents – and so the pattern goes on.

The network of many families is stretched now to the point where their significant relationships are non-existent.

How we handle our relationships links into everything else in our lives. Relationships are the basis for all we are and all we do. History has shown that, with good relationships around them, people can survive almost anything; but in isolation or in a network of dysfunctional relationships, we each become very vulnerable. The Good Childhood report, published in 2009, identified the increasing individualist attitudes in society as damaging to children.

All that we have said about materialism and the entertainment values of our culture might not represent much danger if all our children were living within steady relationships and consistent standards. But they are not. This is why many parents have very little idea of what their children are watching, what products are enticing them to spend their money, or even where they are getting their money from. Given the frailty of some relationships, asking those questions of children would come across as intrusive and provocative.

Trapped at home

For the same reason the home has become a place of great risk for many children. Not only are children free to watch television programmes, DVDs and internet content which they are not yet old enough to cope with, but for an unknown number the perversion of the sexual images they see is lived out in the horror and guilt of their own experience. Just how many children live through years of sexual abuse in their own homes with trusted and respectable relatives can never be accurately known. There are arguments that support the theory that, as child abuse is now much more in the public arena than before, it may not be increasing. Some research suggests that 15-20% of children will be abused by the time they reach 18. However, in a society where the emphasis is on individual choice and the focus is on ownership rather than relationship, child abuse can be rife yet undetected.

To try to keep our children safe from harm, our society has brought in regulations in order to be able to check the past history and criminal record of people who work with children, and laws to give it power to act against those who used to guarantee the safety of the majority of children – because they can no longer be trusted.

10 ways in which most children have not changed

good at friendship

strong sense of fun

full of curiosity

ready to explore

eager for information

loyal

respond to love

optimistic

helpful

energetic

The value of
relationship

No-one to follow

In our culture we are watching a whole generation of young people who are desperate for positive role models.

- They do not have them in the older generation because of these detached relationships, and because of child safety concerns.

- They do not have them in their own generation because most of their pop and sport idols are corrupted by the very materialism our young people aspire to.

- They feel that their parents do not realise how radically the world has changed in the last generation.

- And their grandparents, who do see the change, are revolted by it and blame the young for it.

In every generation we have needed safe people who with real charisma are saying 'Follow me!' We have deprived the new generation of this. This has lead to fast fluctuations of fashion and cult, and to a lack of commitment and direction. How does anyone know whether the present direction is worthwhile if no-one has gone ahead and led the way?

Relationship pressure

We would be naïve if we thought that children were immune from the pressure to form pre-sexual relationships with others. Children see sexual images all the time, they are exposed to films and TV storylines about relationships, and they see their older siblings getting into physical relationships at a very early age. Some children aged 11 or under are sexually active.

- Children are encouraged to dress and behave as adults, and take on adult relationship characteristics.

- Having a boy or girlfriend is encouraged by adults and peers.

- The 'If it feels good, do it' mantra permeates the world of the young.

- An exclusive relationship meets an emotional need of a child who is starved of love.

Are the leaders lost?

We are all affected by this. We are part of this culture; it is our culture and theirs. As leaders we too are deeply affected by materialism with its ease of ownership and emphasis on the collectable.

- We are scared by the culture in which children now live although we created it.

- We too are deeply influenced by the world of advertising both in buying products for identity, and in taking on the more subtle messages about sex, sexual orientation, gender and values.

- We have also changed our standards in the world of entertainment in the last 20 years – seeing and listening to things which now seem ordinary but which at one time would have been sensational in some way or other.

We are our culture – and if we ignore this fact, we will find ourselves finding fault with the new generation in a way which is both hypocritical and irresponsible.

The God who relates

The basis for good communication is good relationships. That is the basis on which God works.

- In a culture where there is a desperate lack of dependable relationships, we have opportunity on our side. If you can offer to the children in your community good, committed, dependable, unconditional relationships you will never have a lack of interest.
  That is what God offers them.

- The new generation is hungry for these reliable relationships. They are already saturated with the new technology (if you want something technical operated at church, a young person will be the expert). But what they are deprived of is personal communication which is just for them – not for the whole nation on the box, nor the whole world on the Web, but for them. They want something communicated to them by someone who cares about them, who sees them as a person who is important.
  That is what God offers them.

- And they need the additional knowledge that if they don't listen today and they come back tomorrow you will be that same committed person and will communicate it again just to them because they are still important.
  That is what God offers them.

Their culture will ensure that they play it cool, never say 'Thank you' and certainly never let on that they need you. That would be weak and their peer group would despise them for it. But the work of the Holy Spirit will be working and teaching them that this is what God is like.

If you are to be God's person in this situation, He needs you to be a whole person – so that as you build relationships with the children around you and share your life with them, He will be revealing Himself through you as someone quite different from everything else on offer.

Notes

Abuse checklist

Child abuse is not simply something to do with sexual or physical abuse. Children are open to abuse in many ways, and we all have a duty to help children who are subject to abuse. High profile cases of children being abused and neglected have resulted in numerous enquiries and changes in the way children are protected and cared for. Your church or denomination should have a Child Protection policy in place which gives thorough details of what to do when a child appears to be being abused or confides in a leader, and you should make yourself familiar with it. The information below is only a general guide.

Aims of the legislation

The Children Act in 1989:

- makes children's welfare a priority
- recognises that children are best brought up with their families wherever possible
- aims to prevent unwarranted interference in family life
- requires local authorities to provide services for children and families in need
- promotes partnership between children, parents and local authorities
- improves the way courts deal with children and families
- gives rights of appeal against court decisions
- protects the rights of parents with children being looked after by local authorities
- aims to ensure that children who are looked after by local authorities are provided with a good standard of care.

Children have rights

The Act also gives children **rights**:

- to be protected
- to be listened to
- to be consulted when a local authority is deciding what should happen to their future
- to be told their rights
- to talk about any worries they have or to make a complaint if things go wrong
- to be helped by the local authority if they will suffer without help or if they have a disability and need help
- to be protected if they are in danger or at risk of harm in any way
- to have their voice heard in some court cases which are about them
- to have their own solicitor and to be able to instruct them about what they want to happen (if they are old enough to understand)
- to say no to being medically examined or assessed (if they are old enough to understand)
- to be told certain things by the local authority if they are in care

---

Abuse checklist

What should you do if a child talks to you about a situation of abuse which they are experiencing?

Try to avoid saying:

- why? how? when? where? who?
- are you sure?
- why didn't you say before?
- I can't believe it.
- this is really serious/don't tell anyone/I am shocked.
- false promises.

As you listen:

- thank the child for telling.
- tell the child that you believe them.
- tell the child what you are going to do and as far as is possible what is going to happen next.

What to do next:

- ensure that the child is out of danger.
- assess whether the child is safe to go home.
- ensure that you give the child your continuing support and friendship.
- seek help and advice from the named child protection person or another appropriate person.
- follow your own church's policy for children's work and child protection. Also speak immediately to the senior minister or to a senior member of your denomination, and inform Children's Services if necessary.

Life at school

This Unit introduces you to the world of the modern school and draws conclusions from this about how we need to run our children's groups in the church today.

Contents

Back to school

In this Unit we are going to look at the educational world of the child. It is hard to define the boundaries of a child's education, since a child's education really encompasses the whole breadth of their life. But the nursery, playgroup and the school gives a clear focus for this education. It is here that the child is offered a view of life – a view which may or may not be the worldview held by their parents or sustained by their home.

So there is a very important piece of experience that you must have in order to complete this Unit. Ideally you need to have spent time in a Primary School recently. A target time would be five half-days, perhaps spread out over two weeks. As an absolute minimum, you should ensure at least six hours of child contact time, in periods of at least 90 minutes. If this is not possible for practical reasons, spend as much time as possible talking with both primary-age children and teachers.

However you arrange it, you need thinking time between periods of contact time, so make a space to think things through. If you simply do one school day, you will come home saturated by the experience and find it difficult to analyse what happened and what you felt about it.

Planning ahead is vital. The school will need to be approached properly with your request. You may have children of your own at the school and know that they welcome parental support. Your minister may need to write a letter explaining the reason for your interest. If you are studying *Leading Children* as a course with a tutor, you will find more information on this in the Student Guide, including a sample letter. Most schools welcome visitors but all will be understandably suspicious if someone approaches them without the right introductions, checks, and so on.

If a visit to a school proves impossible you will need to find a suitable alternative such as a local authority youth club, another church, homework club or playscheme. Your observations will need to be adapted to suit the situation.

The school should have the opportunity to meet you before your first contact visit, and you should take with you the list of questions opposite so that they can see the sort of thing you are hoping to experience. They may have other questions to suggest, reflecting current issues in the school – ask them about this. Remove from the list any questions they express reserve about. The school's cooperation and confidence in you is much more important than using the 'correct' questions.

Remember that you are in school as a visitor and even though you will be of help as an extra pair of hands, the school is doing you a favour. Also try to respect the privacy and space of the staff room, and keep anything you hear or see about individual children confidential. Make sure that everything you write down and have with you about the school is positive and pleasant.

> If you do not understand the world of school, you will not understand a way of life that profoundly influences each child you relate to.

1. How many children and staff are in the school and how are they divided into classes?

2. How is the school day structured? Is there a central timetable covering the whole time or are certain subjects timetabled and other times left more flexible?

3. How much choice and decision is left as the responsibility of the child for the use of their day?

    None   15 minutes a day   30 minutes a day

    An hour a day   An hour and a half a day   Two hours a day

4. Find three positive words which indicate the atmosphere of the school.

    _____   _____   _____

5. Find three positive words which indicate the relationship between staff and children.

    _____   _____   _____

6. List ten different methods of facilitating a child's education – e.g. use of TV, interactive whiteboards, books, computer, discussion.

-                         •
-                         •
-                         •
-                         •
-                         •

7. List ten different questions you hear children asking.

-
-
-
-
-
-
-
-
-

8. When are children with others of an age-group different from their own?

9. Which subject areas are different from those which you explored at the same age?

10. Who enjoys being in school the most – the younger children, older children, head teacher, administrative staff, parents, teaching staff, part-time staff – or a visitor like you?

Other reflections:

Education for life

You should now be quite familiar with what goes on in a modern primary school. You may rather like it, or you may look at modern educational practice and say, 'Not like it was in my day'. Either way, the important questions to ask are:

- What is education?

- How does it happen in schools today?

- How does it affect the relationship between the church and the child?

If only the church, children's leaders and children's evangelists had been asking those questions consistently over the last 30 years, the relationship between the church and children today would be very different.

The truth is that the church has been negligent, and therefore found itself left behind in knowing answers to these questions. As a result, there is a gulf between what happens in school and what happens within the church, even those parts of the church specifically designed for children. Many children's leaders would be amazed if they saw the children from their groups during a normal school day.

What is education?

Chambers Dictionary gives this definition for the word education:

Bringing up or training as of a child: instruction:

strengthening of the powers of body and mind: culture.

Education is not simply learning to write, or to count, or to read. It is true that those skills are crucial, and it is easy to see why they have become the focus of education. But education has never been simply the '3Rs', even in settings where those were the three skills which were tested to ascertain whether the process of education had taken place successfully. Education has always been the big, wide scene of 'bringing up or training' the whole person for the whole of life. Training is simply working towards learning a skill, whereas education is so much more than that.

The book of Proverbs is full of advice about the process and practice of education of the young. It talks of Wisdom as a human being, and describes her calling out in the street to the young. She is vying for their attention with their peer groups and especially with their romances. Life has not changed!

Sacred and secular

Of course, for the Israelites there was never such a thing as 'secular education'. Everything was sacred and the 'education system', which taught children to count their sheep or bolts of cloth, also taught them God's laws and God's Word. Even in more recent centuries schools were set up to educate children in the Christian faith as well as helping with literacy and numeracy.

Once sacred and secular education are differentiated, the secular only seems to have meaning and purpose for:

assessment: We can see the emphasis in our own educational system on assessed tasks. This emphasis has always been there although it is now much more public in the National Curriculum.

employment: In older pupils we see the lack of appetite for education in areas of the country where unemployment is high.

A good theology of education would remove these. The assessment would be there as a personal issue – an answer to the question, 'How am I doing about what I have purposed in my own heart to do?' And the incentive would be there because the purpose would be to learn to live a good and wise life even in the absence of employment.

One reaction to this divide recently has been the growth of demand for schools with a particular religious ethos. Many faith groups are demanding their own schools within our culture. Although there is sometimes political reluctance to grant permission for this, many schools are in fact known to be of one faith or another. There are also many private schools which have been set up with a similar aim. We may look at these schools and feel concern for the limited range of teaching skills or variety of relationships which a small school can provide. But it is important to see that they are trying to address the problems that arise when education is undertaken as a secular activity.

Bible viewpoint

Read Proverbs chapters 1 & 2. See the lack of distinction between the sacred and the secular.

Then read Deuteronomy 11:18-21. See the lack of distinction between the home and school.

Now read Luke 2:41-52. Do you feel you understand this confusing story differently now?

Education and work

Young people who are struggling with unemployment tell us that this has made a nonsense of all that has happened to them since they went to school at the age of five. Of course our culture also has a poor theology of work, but if the divide had not been made between secular and sacred education – if we had taken our Western model from the Hebrews and not the Greeks – how different our present situation would be.

Interview a group of children about their hopes and aims. Then interview some teenagers about their dreams and aspirations for the future. How likely do you think it is that they will achieve their aims? Write some notes here.

The modern school

Tradition

Before the 1960s, the educational style of our schools was formal and uncreative, with children sitting still and listening for a large part of the day (or at least appearing to do so!). Education was something which was done TO us.

We were then tested to see how well we had fulfilled our part of the arrangement – the learning. Where the process had apparently been unsuccessful, there was never any doubt that there was fault on our side and this was then punished. The aim was to ensure that greater effort was made by the child to learn, or to 'be educated'.

The way to satisfy our teachers was to reproduce what they had taught us in the form in which they had taught it. When we gave the right answers, these were ticked to show they coincided with the answers given us in the teacher's examples or that our method of acquiring the answer had matched the method taught in the examples.

Handwriting was copied to re-create the exact image on the page; pages of sums were completed to acquire numeracy skills; the sounds which went with certain written symbols were learnt and put together into words. Alongside these we learnt all the exceptions to the rules, so that we would not be caught out when life appeared not quite as tidy as in the easy examples.

Revolution

In the 1960s and 1970s educational times changed. The magical phrase 'learning by experience' was on the lips of all students at teacher training colleges. Many people went through bizarre teaching practices where the style of teaching and the method of learning in classrooms was radically and shockingly different from what went on in any other class in the school.

Children were suddenly cut free from the confinements of previous methods; some of them were as confused and bewildered as members of the staff room. Teachers asked for their opinions; they were free to choose the pattern of their educational days; and nothing was ever marked wrong (with a cross)!

As with most things in the educational world, we had gone from one extreme to the other – with the maximum of hassle.

Jargonbuster

Year: Continuous numbering of the 13 full years of education, starting from infants to sixth form. For the rough age of the child, add 5. So 'Year 5' children are around 10 years old.

Key Stage: Major milestones in a child's education, effectively breaking the school career into five blocks:

> Foundation stage: Nursery and reception
> Stage 1, years 1-2
> Stage 2, years 3-6
> Stage 3, years 7-9
> Stage 4, years 10-11

SATS: the process of testing children at specific ages, to gauge progress and attainment.

OFSTED: Office for Standards in Education, which inspects schools. The term is usually used for the inspection itself.

INSET: In-service training for teachers. Usually a day off for pupils.

Statementing: the process of gaining an external assessment of a child with special needs ready for appropriate education.

Balanced?

Where are children now in the spectrum of this swinging pendulum? Many would say that they are in a place of excellence of education in terms of content, although there is always more to do and a need for more finance. The excellence is rarely talked about. Nonetheless, it is true that today most children experience a high standard of education with the best of both sides of the pendulum.

Gone are the days when children had no say in their own education; it is no longer something which is done to them, but rather something for which they are asked to take responsibility and make a commitment to.

No longer is there one answer produced for endless exam papers – but opinion, research, debate and variety in the curriculum. Children even have a say in how the school runs through School Councils.

Not for our children the solely cerebral experience of academic learning, because this is partnered by imaginative teaching methods which look for a creative, sensual response as well as a disciplined, scholastic one.

The National Curriculum is aimed at standardising these high aims across the country. It managed to fall foul of most educationalists because of approach and delivery, not because anyone is against its aim.

Those involved in education want the best possible opportunities to be available for the maximum number of children. Politicians have not always made the best decisions about the way these high aims can be achieved in terms of staffing and of finance. Our teachers have not been the only ones to suffer through the frustration of implementing this new curriculum. Children have also suffered as schools have been closed or teachers' support has been withdrawn.

Interview with a teacher

Q: *How do school financial resources affect the child?*

A: There are always more resources needed and a 'need' no longer gives the right to 'help'.

Q: *What about children with Special Needs then?*

A: Statementing can be slow and children find it hard to move to schools with appropriate facilities.

Q: *How have you seen changes in the children themselves over the years?*

A: They know more about the sad side of life before they are able to cope with it – perverted sex, violence and horror. Often they don't know what to do with the knowledge. They seem to have lost the ability to be a child.

Q: *The National Curriculum has brought some really good things hasn't it?*

A: Yes, but the school year is now ruled by SATS. Children are being tested and measured in a public way even when they are very young. They know if they have failed – they know if their school has 'failed its Ofsted'. They feel in some way responsible.

Q: *How possible is it for teachers to reassure children on a continual basis?*

A: The higher the class size, the harder it is for teachers to have a good relationship with each child. Bullying even on a casual, open level is common, although most schools try to keep a lid on it. Discipline at home has definitely changed and there are more discipline problems for all of us than ever before. Some staff feel there is nothing they can do to control a class – the child can do anything and the teacher can do nothing without the parent and the law coming down on them.

Problems -
and opportunities

Family Expectations

Families are aware of their rights, expect choice, and are shy of commitment.

Think of three different ways you would expect to:

show you respect their rights

1

2

3

provide the level of appropriate choice

1

2

3

model committed relationship

1

2

3

The results of
change in education

First the
BAD news...

1. Rights

One of the results is that the word 'rights' is now part of our attitude to ourselves and our surroundings. We hear of 'the rights of the child' and 'the rights of the parent' and (very occasionally...) 'the rights of the teacher'. People in the arena of education now look closely at what they are going to get out of it, and compare this with what they feel they ought to get out of it.

This makes a difference to the reception given to our children's group or club. It is now the right of the parent to expect a certain standard of behaviour and provision for their child. Parents will expect the leaders to be suitably trained and appropriately checked. The modern church group is a contract or agreement between the church and the parent; it is no longer a philanthropic provision for which thanks or appreciation is necessarily appropriate. This makes a big difference to the group, to the relationship of the group to the home, and to the relationship between the child and the leader.

2. Choice

Another result has to do with the expectation of the child in relation to the content of what is taught. Children are used to being interested. They are used to having choices to make throughout their waking day. They are used to being active – or at least to being able to choose whether they are active or not. They are more used to negotiation about behaviour than about 'doing as they are told' without question.

This makes a big difference to the feel of a children's group. The leaders may feel vulnerable and not in control. They may feel that what the church can provide on a limited (or non-existent) budget cannot even start to keep children interested or to compete with the other bids for their time and energy. There are all sorts of opportunities for children outside the timetable of a school day. Often their diaries are busier than those of their carers. It's hard for the church to produce a programme which will seem attractive set alongside the sporting, entertainment and educational opportunities available in many communities. However, given suitable time and resources, the church can offer a credible alternative.

3. Commitment

A third major effect is that regular commitment to a group or membership of a club is not part of our modern culture. Schools now have to work hard to build the loyalty and commitment factor which has been almost automatic in past eras. Although in late childhood the 'belonging factor' is as present as it ever was, the culture of our time pulls against it.

Established organisations like Brownies and Cubs talk today of a radical drop in numbers and a new pattern of belonging which is haphazard in attendance and unpredictable in contribution. Adult leaders, brought up in a different culture, are likely to gauge regulars as the core of the group and test the success of the group by the number of regulars there are. We may need to think of new criteria for success in the light of this different way of being part of a group, and make the most of every session, however many children there are. We certainly need to avoid penalising children for not attending all the time, as many have little control over what they do.

After these three hard implications for our groups, is there anything which might encourage us in our leadership today? Here are a few positives...

...and now the GOOD news

1. Learning for life

Children are now used to a reflective form of education. Teachers use the process of experiential learning in their teaching, and encourage their children to develop this skill. Reflective education is a cycle of learning which moves continually from our experience of life to learning and gathering information, to reflecting on the experience and the learning, to developing action and experimentation, and so creating new experiences for the cycle to begin again.

> This means that the children in your group are not used to being 'told information' and ignoring it. They are used to pursuing information and then reflecting on it in such a way that they make it their own through experience. For the information of faith this is vital – we do not want simply to give information – we are aiming that what the child learns will become part of their life experience. We need to learn not to tell information but to stimulate reflection.

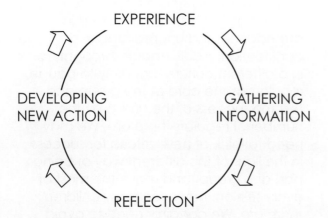

EXPERIENCE

DEVELOPING
NEW ACTION

GATHERING
INFORMATION

REFLECTION

2. The power of story

Narrative has been recognised as an important part in this cycle. Narrative is a powerful way of receiving and giving information; it is also a safe way both to reflect on and to describe experience.

> 'Telling our story' has always been an important part of the Christian message. It is the traditional way in which faith is interpreted for others. It is the method often used by those inside the faith to communicate to those outside the faith. Because of modern education, the children in your group will be used to this method of learning and communication.

3. Time for the child

The relationship between staff and children in schools has been forced to become more detached. The pressure on teachers to deliver the curriculum and keep appropriate records of pupil progress reduces the 'free' time within a school day. Some schools are offering less extra-curricular activities, formerly an enjoyable part of the relationship between adult and child, because teachers who are already working through their lunch hour, after school hours and at weekends are unable to run as many.

> In the smaller group of a church club or group, there can be a level of close relationship and commitment which is not possible now between teacher and pupil in schools. Children are as attracted by committed relationships now as they ever have been, and to have this on offer from the leadership of your group may be a positive counterbalance to the modern scene in schools. Ultimately the church can uniquely offer time and love to children.

Best of both worlds?

Take each 'problem'. How could you minimise its effect on your church group?

1.

2.

3.

Best of both worlds?

Take each 'problem'. How could you minimise its effect on your church group?

Take each opportunity:how could you maximise it in your group?

1.

2.

3.

Parent power

If you are a parent with a child in a primary school, you have a special opportunity to become familiar with the child's experience of school 'from the inside'.

As the demands on staff grow, many schools are looking to their parent body for more support than ever before. There are opportunities for parents to become involved in the life of the school as a regular commitment – through listening to children read, running the library, helping with swimming groups or in regular 'workshop sessions' in the classroom.

You will not only grow your own confidence in communicating with the modern child, but you will also grow your own skills and expertise. Schools are practised at offering a safe and controlled environment in which parental help can be given – you do not need to fear that you will be asked to do something which you are not able to do.

One important way in which involvement like this will help you is that you will see the Children Act regulations and recommendations implemented. You will see it illustrated in school life in a way which could be vital for your own leadership of children's work in the church setting. Most primary school staff will readily answer questions and explain their reasons for what they are doing, so long as you choose your time for questions carefully. It may be worth negotiating a regular time for asking questions and getting the information you need.

Another opportunity for parents to be involved in the life of the local school is as a member of the Board of Governors. Governors of schools have more power and influence than they have ever had before. They also have more responsibility and involvement in time-consuming activities! A caring Christian Governor has a valuable contribution to make to school life – a welcome support to Christian children, parents and teachers. As a governor you have an entrance into the school at almost any time. You will have a say in decisions about money and staffing, the books which are chosen for the library and other resources, themes chosen for school festivals and outings. There are many books available about this role and its responsibilities. It is a position of great responsibility and potential.

The involvement of parents as Governors in schools was a political decision which has had profound effects on education in recent years. As a Christian parent, you have a unique opportunity to resource yourself for work with children, and to contribute positively to the future direction of the school your child attends.

Display

The photographic results from your school visits could be displayed after a church service to give other people the opportunity to see what you are doing in this course. It would also inform them about the life of the local school.

You could pick out some of the photos of children who are known by your congregation and have them enlarged for the display. (Make sure you ask their parents first)

Many older adults see a change in the discipline and attitudes of the young, and draw instant conclusions that everything is bad. This is not true, and whatever we can do to reassure them is valuable for the whole community.

Assignment 4

If you are studying this course with a tutor you must do this assignment.

Comparisons

Complete all three sections of the following assignment. Your written summary should include about 800-1000 words:

1 Try writing down your own school memories and recording them onto a tape. Aim at ten different scenarios between the ages of 5 and 18 years. Write down a few words for each memory, setting it in the context of people and place. Then record your feelings both at the time and now looking back.

2 Interview some children and young people about their experiences of school life. You might do this in the context of your school visits or talk to children from your own church or home environment.

3 Compare the two accounts. What are the striking differences? And similarities?

Send the completed assignment to your tutor for marking by post or email.

Children & the church

This Unit challenges you to think out the place of children within the Christian community and helps you see how to include them in the mainstream of church life.

Contents

The all-age experience

In this Unit we are going to look at the child in relation to the rest of the church – one age-group in a multi-age family.

You may already be involved in the all-age arrangements at your church. In that case you may already have some of the experience referred to in these pages. But look carefully through them to ensure you have reflected on the issues raised, especially regarding the attitudes of church leadership.

You may have limited your involvement with children to when they are in their groups rather than when they are with the rest of the church. You may not anticipate being involved in leading all-age worship, so may think such involvement irrelevant to you. But your children do not live in isolated age-groups like this – they live most of their lives coping with other ages, mostly older than themselves. In a society of fractured relationships it is vital that the church models cross-generational communication. You will understand the child's world better once you have struggled with the joys and frustrations of working with all the age-groups together.

The experiential base for this Unit reflects the two main issues involved in all-age arrangements:

- the attitude and approach of the church leaders.
- the process of putting together sessions (e.g. worship services) which are suitable for people of every age.

All-age leaders?

The success or failure of children's work in a church, and in particular all-age arrangements, depends a great deal on the attitude of the official leaders of the church towards children. If you are to work with children, especially in giving leadership to children's work, it is important that you understand how your particular leaders think about this.

So ask for the opportunity to interview one or more of them. You can record this on tape as you have the conversation, or you can scribble down notes as they answer the questions. If you are doing this course with another leader, one of you can ask the questions while the other records the answers. If you feel adventurous,

borrow a video camera and do a TV-style interview.

The important thing is to record accurately. You will not have time to reflect on the answers and their implications at the time of the conversation – even if you think you will remember – and you cannot go back and ask again!

It is better to ask a few crucial questions and allow plenty of time for the answers, than to rush through a long list where the answers become very superficial. In the box on the next two pages are five questions which you could send to your interviewee before you meet. These will encourage the leader/s you interview to think about the answers they will give, before the actual interview itself.

Making it work

Get involved in planning three all-age sessions for your church. This would be best done as a member of a small group – perhaps with others who are doing the course or who are already committed to the all-age issue. You could discuss with your church staff which would be most appropriate.

Give the three sessions different aims – one could be for worship, one for building relationships, and one for a practical aim (sorting out the church hall, for example). Try to involve different people in the running of the three events, and check with people of different types and ages afterwards about what they have enjoyed and gained from the experience.

> "A despising of true religion when it is found among the very young is a pernicious evil which springs up again in each generation however diligently we may pull up the weed". (Spurgeon)

Questions for leaders

1. What is the best thing about having children and young people attached to the church?

2. What is the most difficult thing about having them?

3. When in your experience are young people most likely to leave the church?

Questions for leaders

1. What is the best thing about having children and young people attached to the church?

4.When do young people become full members of this church?

5. What would you most want children and young people to receive from the church?

A theology of the child

Many people see theology as something for academics to mull their great brains over – a cerebral exercise. There is a place for such theology, and we can thank God for the great theologians we have had over the centuries. But theological thinking is something all Christians do, and theology is not just about what goes on in our brains!

Theology is the way people think about God. It is understanding how God relates to creation, and longing to enter into His thinking about it.

Theology also determines the pattern of our lives. What we each believe about God and creation affects the way we live our lives, at a profound level. This is true for us as individuals, and it is also true for the Christian community as a whole.

Thinking about the poor

Beliefs may look the same but lead to very different outcomes in real life. Often when you look at them more closely, you find that the beliefs are really rather different.

Someone might have a theology that God's Word really matters and that Scripture clearly expresses God's concern for the poor. Their theology will affect the way they think about the poor, and is likely to lead them to express concern for the poor in some practical ways. Looking at Old and New Testament teaching, they may, like Mother Theresa, have a ministry of comfort for the poor.

Someone else might hear God's Word as saying: 'I care for the poor and call my people to bring greater justice to them.' They might then have a ministry of justice in relation to the poor, such as the South American liberation theologies have involved.

Our theology, whether we are academic or not, has practical implications. Theology affects us all.

Thinking about children

A church may have a theology that believes in the care and nurture of the whole congregation, including the next generation. They may then think it vital that the provision for children in the church should be good quality, and will nurture them within the company of the believers. They are likely to be effective in handing on the faith.

Another church's theology may be that the children are the church of tomorrow – who, when they are adults, will become useful and effective disciples of Christ. Such a church will probably only provide a child-minding service with information about the Bible.

Good theology and good practice go hand in hand. The process of theological thinking is:

* we look at the Word of God

* we look at the practice of the church through history

* we observe what is happening in God's world today

* we are involved in the work of the Holy Spirit in that world.

In that way our theology is formed and our practical attitudes, actions and behaviour are governed.

Whatever the number or type of children we have in our church, we must have a strong and clear theology which governs our policy towards them. Our practical application of that theology will need to change all the time, so that God's message has the greatest impact for the children we have – whether they are multi-racial, disabled, highly intelligent, special needs, orphans or from extended families. So the approach will vary, but the theology of the church about children must remain firm.

If our theology says that handing on the faith to the next generation is one of the most vital parts of the church's mission, then the very best should be used for it. We should select the best people and train them thoroughly. We need to budget our resources carefully so that we can provide an environment and equipment that will support the quality of that leadership. And the emphasis needs to be on relationships – because it is people who are communicating the message to people.

Here's a chart to help you gauge how well your church is achieving these ideals:

People chosen for leadership	Depends who offers	Depends who's free	Carefully chosen
Training available	Regularly	Rarely	Never
Quality of environment for children	Not bad	Good	None
Equipment available for church	None	Good	Poor
Relationships between children's leaders	Good	Poor	None

Our theology about children - the way in which the church community thinks about children - will affect the practical ways in which a church expresses concern for them. Make some notes here about your own church.

> Point your kids in the right direction; when they're old they will not be lost.
>
> Know your sheep by name; carefully attend your flocks.
>
> Proverbs 22:6, 27:23 (The Message)

Starting from scripture

Read these three passages from the Bible:
Deuteronomy 11, Psalm 78:1-8, Matthew 18:1-14

If these were the only three passages of the Bible you had read, what would your theology of children be? Try to sum it up in five statements.

1.

2.

3.

4.

5.

What would your practical application of these be in the life of a church?

1.

2.

3.

4.

5.

If someone came into your church and tried to guess what your theology of children was by watching the life of the church, what conclusions would they draw?

1.

2.

3.

4.

5.

The child in your midst

Reflection:

- What are 'childhood's bright epiphanies'?
- What certainties would you want a child to learn from the church?

Spend about 30 minutes thinking and making notes about this.

The Old Testament child

The message about children in the Bible is patchy. It is not set down in one book or series of chapters. Instead it streams through Scripture in threads or themes. One of these themes is 'The children among you' or 'The child in your midst'.

It's a powerful theme. Deuteronomy 11 and Matthew 18:1-14 are good examples.

Throughout Deuteronomy the giving of the law is set in the context of children living as part of the people of God.

> They were to be told of what God had said in the past.
> They were to be told of what God had done in the past.
> Through that they were to come to an understanding of who they were themselves.

It was what God had said and done in the past which gave them their identity! As children living among God's people heard, saw and absorbed all this in the normal course of life, they would come to understand that the promises of blessing and the warnings of judgement were for them too. They, like their parents and grandparents, had to be people of obedience to God.

The children of the Old Testament were not going to be able to say 'I didn't know' and 'It wasn't my fault' – the two classic excuses we all have used throughout our childhood.

Jesus: like a child

When Jesus took the child in Matthew 18, he stood the child among them – not out in front where most children are self-conscious and uncomfortable, nor at the back where they are uninvolved and bored, but right in the middle where they were vital and integral to what was going on. Then Jesus said, 'Here is your model – make sure you live out your faith like this'. Evidence that we have from the early church indicates that families worshipped together and the child was in the centre of all that happened.

The church child today

As we take this theology of the place of the child within the people of God, and apply it in the context of our churches today, we need to find ways of including our children in the church – as a unique group certainly but integral to the whole. Each child needs recognition, rites of passage, teaching and encouragement; they also need to have their practical and spiritual contributions welcomed and received. They need all of that because every person does – and children are people!

Our theology says that God has chosen to relate to, to communicate with, to care for, and to give gifts to his people. Each person is unique in his creation, and God has chosen to entrust to his people the message of salvation. Forgiveness and the life of the Holy Spirit are the blessings of the people of God. They are also given warnings that if they neglect this work of salvation, they stand under the judgement of God. If children are part of God's people, they are a crucial part of this receiving – and this commission – from a generous and almighty God.

Unless we take this theology seriously, our young people will always be an unheard minority within the church. They will grow up learning to live as schizophrenics between two worlds – the world of school/society 'out there' where they are taken seriously, and the world of church where they are not considered mature enough to take an active role. And our church life will be impoverished without the influence and gifts of each new generation.

And the children outside the church?

So the church needs to rethink how it celebrates the Christian life with its children as an integral part of the church. But the church also needs to consider the children who have not yet joined. Evangelism among children needs the same amount of strategic planning as any other age group. We may want to consider what 'church' could be for children in the community – perhaps the after-school club or midweek group is as much church to them as Sunday worship is to 'churched' adults.

The way children learn, the culture they have been born into and are growing up in, the needs they have for committed relationships, for good leadership role-models and for appropriate bridges into the church – all of this is vital for the church to get to grips with. If these issues are ignored, then the future church is that much more likely to be restricted to those who have been born into church families.

Church of tomorrow

The church currently operates with corridor vision where most activities, services and even the buildings are designed for an adult membership between the years of 35 and 65, and where children are seen as 'members-in-waiting'. Of course they don't wait. They leave. Research reported in the book *Reaching and Keeping Tweenagers* (Peter Brierley, Christian Research, 2003) revealed that children leave church around 18 months after they decide to leave.

No new generation has ever had much patience waiting around for the old generation to get its act together. This one is no exception. The real danger now is that, by the time the church realises its own plight caused by ignoring the young, they will have disappeared. The people who had been treated as 'the church of tomorrow' will be just 'the church which might have been'.

Safe in the midst?

Even in the church, children need to be kept safe.

Here too the provisions of the Children Act are important to bear in mind.

CHILDREN IN THE WAY

'If we want children full of faith and active,
Let's start by making church rich and attractive.
We'd better make ourselves attractive too,
In what we preach, yes, and in what we do;
Is adult worship chalk or cheese
Weighed against childhood's bright epiphanies?
We think we have to ape the media hype
And feed our children not red meat but tripe.
In tiny pieces, tasteless, bland, diluted:
The twentieth century stomach isn't suited
To certainties, or truths expressed with vigour,
Or any kind of intellectual rigour.'

A child's Bible

If you can't explain something to a child, you don't really understand it at all.

Explain to a friend (or a study companion) the teaching of Jesus in John 15:1-8.

Now ask them to pretend they are six years old, and explain it to them again. Ask them to interrupt you on any concept or vocabulary which they do not understand.

How does the second explanation differ from the first? Which is more profound? Or more challenging? What is there that prevents this passage from being relevant or applicable to a child?

The all-age church and the all-kinds church

Capacity for believing lies more in the child than in the man. We grow less rather than more capable of faith. (Spurgeon)

What the church says and does about membership, teaching, worship, service and mutual support has vital implications for everyone – men and women, wealthy and poor, able and disabled, and people of every race. The church today is at least aware of many of those issues, and attempting to be inclusive.

But often children and young people are not included in the discussion of such issues. Adults make all the decisions. In baptism, confirmation, holy communion, worship services, teaching, ministry – in all these events, children experience the life of faith as something which is done to them, rather than something in which they participate. They then grow up taking no responsibility for their faith.

One way to counteract this exclusion of children is to create good all-age worship, learning and activities.

'All-Age' is a term which is used of all kinds of events. Some churches use this title when their children are in the adult service for fifteen minutes before going to their own groups; others use it when they have uniformed organisations in the service – instead of 'parade service'. Neither of these does justice to the term.

An event is 'all-age' when people of all ages are in the same place for the same purpose for the same length of time.

An all-age service – whether of the Word or of the Eucharist – will be prepared on the basis that every person, of whatever age, has a place in it and is expected to give and receive during it.

An Anglican baptism promise

We welcome you into the Lord's family.

We are members together of the body of Christ.

We are children of the same Heavenly Father.

We are inheritors together of the Kingdom of God.

We welcome you.

Tell me, and I'll forget.

Show me, and I'll remember.

Involve me, and I'll belong.

Chinese proverb

"The truth which God has given us about himself – Father, Son and Spirit – remains true for all age-groups not just for adults. The urgent task is to find a way of conveying it which does justice to the message and its hearers alike."

(Francis Bridger)

Look at the potential

All-Age services and events are exciting in their potential. Here are ten positive effects of running such events, from my own experience:

1 They give a clear message that every individual, no matter what their age or ability, is important to God and vital to the church.

2 They give clergy a clear need and opportunity to use lay people – a huge variety of gifts need to find expression in such a service.

3 They require a group to work together preparing and planning the service – and usually having fun!

4 Since those people all have to understand Scripture themselves before leading others into it, the group is always on a learning curve.

5 Because the service is for everyone, it cannot rely only on speaking and listening. At its best it will be visual and interactive – providing opportunity not only to teach the Bible in creative ways but for creative responses from the participants.

6 They are ideal services to use as an introduction for the 'unchurched' because the faith is explained for children – without making a lot of assumptions about what people 'know' already.

7 People attending these services are (usually…) more relaxed; so the service provides the opportunity to teach new music and to try out other new ways of 'being church'.

8 It can be a time when church leaders and church members get to know each other better.

9 It is an excellent opportunity for evangelism to whole families – and for Christian families to invite their neighbours.

10 It gives the opportunity for the church to teach the big issues of Christian life and doctrine in a non-academic way to the whole membership.

What's the idea?

When a group comes together to plan an all-age event, whether it is to be a service of worship and teaching or a church fun day, the one thing that may create panic is the lack of ideas.

Here are five important ways to prepare ideas for an all-age event:

1 Invite people onto the planning group who will understand the spiritual aim of what you are doing and who will be prayerfully committed to the group and its task. Keep the planning group small – you can always involve others afterwards, by delegating jobs and roles.

2 Meet regularly, rather than trying to prepare everything in one evening! And agree beforehand how you will prepare for each planning meeting. If people come to a meeting 'cold', you will waste a lot of time and anyone who is feeling inadequate will have that feeling confirmed.

3 Start with the Bible passage or the Christian theme, not with the good ideas for activities or visuals. One person might prepare a basic introduction to the theme. Read the Bible passage together and pray and chat it through informally. Have a basic but reliable commentary available to help resolve debate about its meaning. If you get excited about God's Word, you will end up with a good event.

4 Collect together a few books which give practical ideas. These may be books about All-Age Worship, or books about using the Arts with children. Have these books around to browse through if you get stuck. Remember that other people's ideas will need to be adapted to your situation.

5 Take it in turns to write down a list of what has been decided and who is going to do what. Then you can refer back to this when you need to, and nothing will be forgotten or need to be planned all over again.

More?

For a detailed workbook on the process of 'theological reflection' today, see **God Thoughts: A starter course in theological reflection**, by Ian Aveyard (St John's Extension Studies)

Ask the children

Children will be very used to being consulted about their wants and needs at school and in any clubs and groups they attend. Yet the church has traditionally been very poor at asking children for their views.

Look through the timetable of a week or a month in the life of your church community. Make a timetable of events for all age-groups and then highlight those which are for under-11's (or where that age-group would be welcomed and catered for).

Then think of some ways in which children could have a higher priority in the worshipping community of your church.

Now get together a small group of people from your church who represent the different child age-groups. Provide refreshments and an informal atmosphere. Ask them for suggestions of how the church could be more welcoming to children. You may need to ask the small children separately, since the discussion group would be a difficult forum for them to make a contribution.

Lastly, ask for a slot in the next meeting of the decision-making leadership of your church, to talk about children in the church.

- Take your timetable results with you.

- Show them your suggestions for raising the profile of children in the church.

- Ask them what their plans are for children and young people in the church for the next 10 years.

- Ask them how the leadership team for youth and children can be brought into the conception of such plans.

- Leave behind a copy of the survey you have completed, and a copy of your suggestions, for each member of the group.

For further thought.....

These books may help:

The first four chapters of *A Church for All Ages* by Peter Graystone and Eileen Turner (Scripture Union, 1993) are very readable on this. This is currently out of print – please contact the Extension Studies office if you would like a photocopy of this.

Have a look at *All Age Everything* by Nick Harding (Kevin Mayhew Ltd, 2001), *Top Tips for All Age Worship* by Nick Harding (Scripture Union, 2005), and Grove/CPAS Booklet *Body Beautiful*.

Another really useful book is *Reclaiming a Generation* by Ishmael (Children's Ministry 2001). Read especially the chapter on 'The Family Church'.

Spend some time thinking about why it is a good thing for the church to spend some of its time all-together.

Read through these passages from the Bible: Psalms 1, 39, 104, 148, Ecclesiastes 3, Mark 13.

1. What impression does the Bible want to give about the passing of time?

2. What images does it use?

3. Draw some of them or write the words in felt-tip pens.

4. Write down five cautions the Bible might want you to make to those whose time alive is still ahead of them.

Assignment 5

If you are studying this course with a tutor you must do this assignment.

Sharing ideas with church leaders

After you have worked through Unit 6 and met with your church leaders, write up some reflections on the process in about 500 words.

Send in everything (your survey, suggestions and reflections) to your tutor for marking by post or email.

Products of family life

This Unit helps you reflect on the realities of family life today, including your own. There are many implications from this for our work with children, and we explore some of these.

Contents

Who's in the cupboard?

Clustered around each individual child is a group of people. This is their family.

It used to be easier to define 'family', as all a small child's immediate and intimate people were related to them. Mother, father, brothers and sisters, grandparents, cousins – these and many others made up a child's first 'community'. Today, with the demise of the extended family and the frequent breakdown of the nuclear family, a child's network of intimate relationships may have little to do with the people that child is actually related to. But the concept is the same. 'Family' is that network of people we are born into. Even if the child is in a foster home, that 'family' is real and will continue to have a profound influence on the child throughout their life.

As a children's leader, you may see a small proportion of a child's family network quite frequently. These are the immediate carers, normally parents or step-parents, but often others – like a grandmother playing a quasi-mother role for a young single mother to enable her to work.

But behind the few you see frequently, there will be a host of others, people who have played a part in the child's first 'community' and have helped to shape who they are. Some of this 'family' will no longer be alive. But despite being invisible to us, they are carried around in the heart and mind of the child, sometimes consciously, sometimes not.

To be prepared to complete this unit, you need to have a sensitive understanding of this family reality. No matter how experienced you feel about such things you should still complete two pieces of research about the family. If you are aware of these realities already, it won't take you long – and it's surprising what you learn!

What's in a tree?

Do some investigation about family trees. This need not be time-consuming or involve long visits to a graveyard. All you need to do is to ask three different people what they know about their family tree. Choose people of different ages and backgrounds, and try not to fall back on neat and tidy family structures, as many children are not in such family networks. Use a simple format like this the one on the next page:

☐ Fill in as many spaces as possible with the name of the relative (or quasi-relative) and a description of the relationship they have with the person you are interviewing.

☐ Use one colour of highlighter to show people who have died (it is easy to lose sight of these people, or underestimate their influence).

☐ Use another colour to indicate those relatives the child feels particularly close to.

My family tree

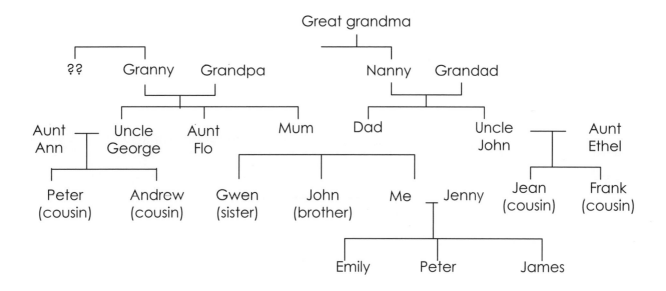

A family visit

Interview a family together. You will find this easier if it is a family where you know more than one member before the interview, but you don't need to know them all.

As with the leadership interview (see page 89-90), you can do this like a reporter, taking notes, or you can use audio or video recording to keep a record of what is said. An audiotape is probably best for this, if you can position the microphone so that it picks everyone up adequately. It frees you from taking notes, so the conversation can flow freely, and it is less obtrusive and distracting than a video camera.

Explain why you are interviewing the family. In particular, make it clear what you are doing with the recording, and who else if anyone will hear it (if you are doing this preparation with someone else, the family needs to know that your study companion will hear the tape too). Agree with them when the tape will be erased, or offer to send them the tape when you have finished your course. You will need to make these agreements if you expect a family to be honest with you about their relationships.

Write down beforehand what questions you will ask. Below are some suggestions, but there are many other approaches which would still give you good insight into how a family 'works'.

You might like to take a photograph of the family group.

> Is there a time when you are usually all together?
>
> When would be the worst possible time to have an unexpected visitor?
>
> What sorts of things make you cross with each other?
>
> Is there one of you who usually acts as peacemaker?
>
> Which is a better time for your family – first thing in the morning or last thing at night?
>
> Is there someone who usually sets the mood for the family?
>
> Do you all get on better when you are on holiday – or is it the opposite?
>
> What's the best thing about being a family?
>
> What's the worst thing about being a family?
>
> If you could have more of one thing in order to be a happier family, what would it be – money, bathrooms, holidays, bedrooms, cars, phones, etc.?

Family is

The word 'family' evokes a whole range of emotions in our culture. The possible patterns for 'family life' and the structure of the family are flexible and fluid as never before.

Many people condemn the modern view of family and blame it for a lot of the moral decay and poor social values we see in society today. There are some families that are stuck in a cycle of poor parenting and bad family relationships which seem to continue from one generation to another.

Is family experience really as bleak as the statistics indicate? Who knows what goes on behind the closed doors of our family homes? We all know an example of an unhappy, dysfunctional family, but we all know an example of a thriving and contented family too.

Are these family?

The possible settings for 'family' to happen in, are listed in *Something to Celebrate*, Church of England Synod report (Church House Publishing, 1995) as:

- stepfamilies
- married couples and children
- married couples without children
- lone parent families
- single person households
- elderly people
- lesbian and gay partnerships
- extended families
- families & ill/elderly relative
- families without work
- homeless families
- student/young adult households
- foster families
- widows/widowers
- families and friends

Statistics

- The number of births registered outside marriage rose from 81,000 in 1981 to 220,000 in 1990.

- In 1990, 80% of the children born to women under 20 were born outside the context of marriage.

- In one survey, 40% of engaged couples did not expect their marriage to last (Wedding and Home magazine)

- Research done by Peter Brierley for MARC Europe into reported sexual abuse to children can only horrify those who care for children today.

Whatever the research figures, it is obvious to the most casual observer that family life has changed in its patterns:

- Some families live with one partner permanently working abroad.

- Some families care for their children by one partner working nights and the other partner working days.

- Some families are trapped into an annual house move as one parent moves up the promotion ladder of their employment.

- Some families consist of a lone parent with frequently-changing partners.

- Some families expect children to care for themselves while the adults are ill, or controlled by drug or alcohol addictions.

- Some families have one parent living with the children, while the other struggles to sustain relationships with the children through allotted access time.

Does it matter? Is one pattern much better than any other? Does it make any difference to the children involved? Does it make any difference to the work and ministry to which we are committed with children in and through the church?

belonging

Belonging

The deepest need that human emotion recognises is the need to belong. Whoever we are and however we have been brought up and educated, there is a ringing question deep in our being which says, 'Where is my place to be?' Ideally that place is inhabited by those who recognise my place and celebrate the fact that I am occupying it – it is not a vacuum or a desert island, or a place characterised by hostility and aggression.

- Draw out a map of the main areas of your life (home, work, leisure, wider family, friends, etc).

- Mark in each 'area' the people who share that space with you.

- Describe what your role is in each area (mother, boss, organiser, maverick, carer, etc.).

- Assess the level of belonging you feel in each area.

- What seems to be the vital ingredient which affects how much you feel you 'belong'?

The children who come to our groups, whether they are the children of church families or those who are experiencing their first tenuous links with the church, will be searching for ways in which to meet their need to belong.

- Some of them will be happily confident of their place in their family, their school, their circle of friends and in the church congregation. If all of this is true then they are likely to come confidently into your group and have as much to contribute as you have.

- Many others will already have felt the pain of not belonging in several areas of their lives. They will be wary of the group – it might prove to be yet another disappointment. If we are insensitive to their needs and presume that all children are entering into a relationship with us at the same pitch of confidence, we will cause damage and hurt.

Clustered around every child there is a group of unseen people – people who by one definition or another are part of their family. We may catch a glimpse of them bringing or fetching the child, asking us questions about time and place. Some we may know by face or even by name – they may be members of a church group or parents of children who are friends with our own.

Almost certainly, we will know very little about this unseen family – their attitudes towards marriage relationships, their financial situation, their attitudes to sex and power. It is important that we tread with care into a relationship with their child. The child has crucial day-to-day relationships with that cluster of unseen people; it is the group to whom they will look in the first instance for satisfaction for their need to belong. It is vital that – as we relate to them, recount the Bible to them, pray with them and listen to them – we do nothing which would in any way damage that cluster of belonging relationships. We must be careful not to make judgments about particular forms of family that seem unusual to us or condemn the adults who care for the children we work with.

A child hit out at another in the Sunday group during an argument over the crayons. When the leader explained that hitting out is wrong, the boy replied "But me dad tells me to hit anyone who gets in my way".

The view from here

A child's background and sense of belonging make a fundamental difference to the way in which they interpret the Bible and hear its message.

Read these three Bible stories: Genesis 27, 2 Samuel 11, Luke 10:38-42

- How might a secure, well-loved child understand each narrative?

- How might each be understood by a child experiencing sexual abuse by a relative?

- How might each be understood by a child whose parents are in two separate homes?

You and me

We all carry baggage from our experience of family during our childhood and adolescence. We may have felt loved and encouraged, or unable to meet the high expectations of those around us.

What links can you see between your understanding of family at the time of your childhood, and God's approach to you as you came to faith?

You will need to look a these notes when you do the assignment at the end of this Part

A place of safety

Some children have grown a strong and healthy inner sense of belonging. Others are confused about where they belong or how they feel about belonging where they do. It is important that we relate appropriately to these very different children, and learn to spot the symptoms of a weak or unhappy set of bonds at home.

One way in which we get clues about this is by listening to a child's rules for life. They will have grown these through their experience of home, school and other areas of their life. If we listen to the way in which the child speaks about their family or their friends, their teachers and their neighbours, we will be able to form an impression of what that set of values or rules is. It will help us to know how the child feels about themselves – and about us. It will also help us to see the church and hear the Bible through their eyes and ears – not so that we change the message but so that we communicate it in an appropriate way.

In the church, we teach God's rules to people, but in relating to children, it is important that we listen to their rule structure too. If we don't, we will be putting them in a dilemma where they are torn between two opposing demands.

Notes

The value of rules

The rules of any group are important – they keep danger out and they give the group a sense of identity.

Today many Christian families are wary of setting rules for the family by saying, "We do this or that". They seem afraid to set boundaries in case the child rebels against them. But without the rules the child loses a sense of who they are and of this vital place to which they belong.

People cheering on their team at a football match will wear the team shirt, or wave a scarf or banner. This encourages the team – they can identify their supporters – but it also gives the supporters an identity. They belong with that team. Identity keeps you safe within that group because you cannot be muddled up with the opposing team's supporters.

The same is true of family values and rules – its like wearing a uniform and waving a banner. It provides a clear identity and a place of safety. Children will always flex their muscles and rebel against the rules, but when they do, they may be saying one of several things:

"These rules are not appropriate for us or our culture. Let's change them."

"You are setting too high a price for the little identity you are giving me."

"Is this place of safety still there, and are the boundaries keeping it safe really strong?"

"If I go along with all this what do I gain?"

It is unlikely to mean that they want the process of rules and boundaries to be removed altogether.

When home becomes HELL

Some of the children who come into our groups will be people who have been badly let down by their family. The very cluster of people who were supposed to stand with them in that safe place have become the danger which threatens them. Instead of a safe boundary around this family, there is now a barrier – of secrecy, of guilt, of threat – which merely prevents the fearful situation from being detected by those outside.

Some children suffer years of mental, physical or sexual abuse before breaking cover and telling the story. ChildLine and other phone services listen to countless stories of tragic suffering where the only safe person to talk to is the faceless, anonymous person at the end of a telephone. You may know of teachers or social workers who work with children who are in daily danger of neglect, abuse and harm.

We are not anonymous or faceless to the children in our groups. This does not mean that we can be closely involved in such difficult situations, but it does mean we must be alert.

In dealing with such a situation, there are three important 'ground rules':

1 Don't presume that it couldn't happen to this family, or this child, or in this place.

People have got away with abuse down through the centuries by being apparently respectable, law-abiding, even religious people. Many leaders in politics, academia or the church have also been discovered to have abused children, and there is clear connection between abuse and the use of power.

Where children are being unresponsive, uncooperative or downright difficult, there could be a hidden reason for their behaviour. The most important thing we can do for them is to give them a reliable welcome whenever they come to the group. That means giving unconditional and sensitive love in an appropriate manner, and trying to maintain a reliable, consistent relationship every time we are with the children.

2 Remember that most of us are not authorised counsellors and we could exacerbate the damage rather than heal it.

It is easy for us to feel that as we have had a child in our group for (say) two years, we know the child rather well. That is simply not true. Compare the time you spend with them with the amount their class teacher spends with them, or their relations might spend with them.

If you are seriously concerned for a child because of a sudden change of behaviour or because of symptoms of intense withdrawal, it is better to go through an official of the church or to an official person at the local school, than to make any attempt to become involved yourself.

3 Be vigilant about how you and your fellow team members behave.

Children are trusted to our care, and we must take every precaution to keep them safe. We need to be meticulous in the way we select people to be with them and the places where we meet with them.

It is important that you become familiar with the Child Protection Policy issued by your denomination or implemented by your church. If your church does not have such a policy it is clearly in breach of the expectations of The Children Act. All such policies are designed to both protect children and protect those who work with them, and good practice should never be ignored. It only takes one careless episode to produce a situation where a child and a leader are damaged. For more information and advice contact your denominational office or the Churches Child Protection Advisory Service.

We have such an important job to do as children's leaders in the church. It is vitally important that we are seen to do this job to the highest possible standards.

Not us!

Some churches have responded to Child Protection policies negatively by saying that it is too much trouble or that it cannot apply to them because they are only a small group. The truth is that the policies are there to keep you and your children safe from trouble. And laws and recommendations apply to anyone looking after children – however small the group is and however infrequently it meets. This means seeking a Criminal Records Bureau clearance for staff and volunteers.

The children who had been victimised did not come disproportionately from any identifiably social, class, ethnic, religious or racial background. Sexual victimisation was widely and broadly distributed.

David Finkelhor
(A Sourcebook on Childhood Sexual Abuse, Sage, 1986)

The highlights

Look back to the summary of the Children Act on page 69. Use highlighters to help you focus on particular points:

- red = most important items
- blue = things new to you

Any resulting purple items should be written out and stuck on your mirror, so you see them every morning!

Make some notes here:

Follow my leader

The family is meant to be a place where children are safe in the knowledge that someone else is in charge, someone else is responsible, someone else is the leader and they can simply follow. By experiencing good leadership and the wise exercise of responsibility, they come to want to exercise it themselves in a good and healthy way.

But children often become leaders in their own families in a way that exhausts them. In some families the marriage relationship only survives because it negotiates through the children or pivots around them.

- If two adults are struggling to communicate with each other, it will always be easier for them to communicate with their child instead. In the end it can become such a habit that the parents only ever communicate through the child. This can extend beyond the difficult or significant things, to all mundane conversation about their day or what they were just watching on the television.

- If the child is from a previous marriage, their relationship with the two adults in the house is uneven. The stepparent may be anxious to be successful with this new parenting role, and the actual parent is probably feeling guilty about the experience of unhappiness at home that the child has already had. It is then easy to play one off against the other – which is another level of responsibility which the two adults have effectively passed to the child.

- In some homes the child is the unwilling spectator of marriage rows, sees them coming and tries to take the role of peacemaker before the row erupts. The two adults can quickly make a habit of communicating by asking their child questions or giving them information which is really intended for the other listening ears. The child in such situations dare not 'rock the boat' because they instinctively realise that they have responsibility for the well-being of the marriage.

Child reactions

If a child from this kind of daily dilemma comes into membership of our group, they may react in several different ways.

- Some may continue to play the part which has become such a habit – they may make an instant response to any disharmony in the group and seem unable to leave any other two children to disagree.

- Others may be quite the opposite and see your group as their one opportunity to have an argument themselves – since they never dare do that at home.

- Others again may melt into the background, with relief that everything will go on without them becoming involved.

- Some may push themselves forward because they are only used to being the central and important point of any action.

Think about your group members. Can you identify any of these elements in their behaviour?

Adult reflections

We have talked here about children but they are not the only members of your group. There are the adult leaders, like you and me – who were once children.

We also bring into the group the experience of being part of that parental family we had as children. All those experiences are there within us.

- We may be acutely aware that various negative experiences had a great impact on us, or we may have blocked out painful events and they seem hardly memorable today. We may have needed pastoral counselling ourselves to try to resolve some of these.

- Or we may look back on an experience of childhood which in retrospect seems full of sunny meadows and supportive love.

We bring it all with us, healed or hurt, hardly remembered or vividly there. We are what our past has made us, and never more so than in the experience we have had of family life.

This will affect the way we receive children and the way we work with other adults. It will affect the way we teach God as 'Father' and 'Son' and the way we introduce our relationship with God to children. It has played a part in forming our theology.

Two Bible resources

The gospel is for the broken-hearted and it spells out a message of healing and renewal. Every child coming to our group can hear the message of God which always begins 'Come to me and I will…' We may frequently feel inadequate but we need never feel that the message is!

1. Read through Isaiah 61. Write a 100 word letter to an imaginary child who is struggling with a difficult home situation. Explain what you have just read in this chapter, for their comfort and pleasure. Read the letter out loud.

2. Read John 17:6-19. Pick out three key words of truth from this prayer. Repeat them over and over again to a rap rhythm that you could use with children. Try out the rap rhythm by clicking your fingers.

Growing ourselves

It is important that the ministry of being a leader of children leads us continually back to being like a child again. We need to be self-aware enough to know that this will not always be comfortable or easy.

This happens in many ways and is something which a course like this can give space for. But thinking through how family has shaped you and your values is not just something to do on a course – it should be something which happens as a continual and demanding exercise. It is one way in which our ministry with children is the very means which God uses to minister to our own lives.

Such reflection is like a doorway through which God can come and enter an otherwise closed and unused room from our past. It is like a mirror into which we look – expecting to see the child that we used to be, but actually seeing ourselves as we now are. Only as we take time – and allow God time – to show us the vital components which have made us into the people we are today, will we begin to understand ourselves.

When we understand ourselves we will accept the 'hamster wheel' we are sometimes trapped in, or the 'trampoline' from which we always jump. There is nothing wrong with that – we all operate this way. What is dangerous is when we live out our lives – and our leadership of children – in ignorance of the effect our past has on us.

Some optional activities

Belonging

Use a concordance and look up 'belong'. Read the passages which use this word.

Church as family

Ask your church leader what he or she thinks this means. Then think through how that explanation is worked out in the life of your church.

The people of God

Take some photos of the people of God who meet regularly in your church. Ask someone else to take one of the photos so that you are in the picture. Look at the photo and ask yourself how you feel being there. Why is this?

Assignment 6

If you are studying this course with a tutor you must do this assignment.

My family and childhood

Drawing on what you have learnt in this part, write about 800-1000 words about your own family and the influence it has had on your life.

Send the completed assignment to your tutor for marking by post or email.

The magic of creativity

This Unit explores the concept of 'creativity', and how important it is to human existence and to our relationship with God. It is also a key area for common activity between adults and children.

Contents

A child at play

This Unit will explore the creativity of childhood and the role which creativity plays in the life and development of a child – especially of a child's faith.

As with the previous Units, your study really needs to be done against the background of experience. The relevant experience for this Unit is to observe children using the creative arts. You should try to become a 'participant observer', sitting alongside the children and using the materials they are using. You will 'skew' their creative work if they become aware they are being watched – and you will enter into their experience much more if you join them in it.

If you have natural ability in the creative arts, you might want to organise your own creative activity with children and reflect on this. But only do this if you are confident that you will still be free to reflect on the experience and learn from it. Actually arranging the experience can absorb all your attention!

You might be able to arrange for this experience in a local school or playgroup, your own church group, or in a more focused artistic group for children (like a holiday workshop run by a local authority). Again, introductions are important to get the right kind of 'entry' to official activities.

Try to reflect on the creative experience under specific categories, even though experience of the arts is often not clearly divided like this. For example, watching dance involves your appreciation of the movement, of the meaning, of the music and often the colour or design of the set. But the discipline of defining the different art forms enables you to analyse what you are seeing (and what a child is experiencing) more easily when you are beginning to do this as a new skill.

Here are some categories you can use, but create your own if that is more satisfying. Write down the categories you are going to use before you start, even if you later change them. This helps you be specific both about what you are seeing and about what you want to see.

For each of my categories there are some clues about what to look for to 'get into' it.

Drawing and painting

- Look at the way in which ideas are used to inspire this.

- Do any children look unsure of how to begin?

- Who completes quickly and who takes time and care over their work? Are any of the latter showing anxiety about their performance?

- How much do colours matter? And does the shape or colour of the paper make any apparent difference?

Modelling

- How many children simply enjoy the feel of the material – clay, playdough, paper-mache?

- How many announce from the beginning what they will make?

- Do any of them express frustration or inability?

- How successful are the results in your eyes?

Dance and movement

- Look at the patterns used, the ideas which are used to trigger dance, the interaction between the children.

- Take note of those who seem to prefer solitude, and those who look uncomfortable about the experience. Any ideas as to why?

- Look out for the child with natural ability, and/or the one who has taken the lead.

- Consider the role played by the leader or teacher.

- What effect does the venue have on this activity?

Drama and mime

- Look at the ideas which trigger this – are they imposed on the children, or do they grow from the children's own lives and experience?

- Look at the way ideas are grown by the children as they work with them.

- Listen to any speech which is used and the way character is displayed.

- Who looks uncomfortable? Any ideas as to why?

- Consider the role played by the leader or teacher.

- What effect does the venue have on this activity?

General

- Who gives the ideas for this work?

- Which children seem naturally to take the lead, and which are particularly suited to this type of activity?

- What kind of ideas work most easily – stories, poems, or free flow?

- What sort of chat goes on while the children are working?

- How much encouragement do they need to continue to a conclusion?

It is important that you write down something as soon as possible after the experience. This may be single words – perhaps something you overheard or words which were in your own mind as you experienced the creative work. Or it may be a description of one moment of that creative time.

You may be in a position to come away with examples of the results of the children's creativity, but if not, take some photographs or draw sketches which you can look back at as you complete this Unit.

Notes

Christians create

Will they like it?

In an all-age service in your own church, what would be the response of the average member of the congregation to:

- a dramatic presentation instead of a sermon?

- a celebratory dance after the confession or communion?

- projected images illustrating the Scripture reading?

- a percussion band to accompany the reading of a Psalm?

To those who don't like it, what could you say to encourage them to enter into the experience?

Penny Frank writes:

As a child I used to feel envious of God when the story of Creation was read or re-told to me. It was not simply that God had been so successful in everything He had made so that He stepped back each time and said, 'That's good!' It was more that He must have had such a lot of fun doing it!

It really appealed to me as a child – and still does – that God could say the word 'Light' and from that second there was light. It fascinated me that in that very word spoken by the Creator God was the power to produce out of chaos a world of amazing variety – a tropical sun, the frosty late harvest moon at the back of our house, and the sheet of stars which held their place night after night for me to identify. God said the word, and order was brought out of chaos and beauty sprang into the world. What fun!

As a child it seemed such a good idea for the struggle to be taken out of making things. I remember the sympathy I felt for Adam as he is consigned to a life-time of hard labour because of his sin. I felt even more sympathy for myself as I realised that the struggle was what I had inherited too!'

God took a risk in allowing mankind the freedom to choose good or evil. Yet this element of choice is essential if people are to be creative at all. God affirms humanity's freedom and our place as His co-creator (Genesis 2:19-20) by allowing Adam to name the living creatures. The way in which it is described is similar to the wording in a 'Just-So' story.

Sin has not robbed people of their capacity to enjoy and delight in the act of creation. It is the element of hard work and pain which has been introduced by the Fall. The world of images and symbols is necessary for the wholeness of a person.

It is clear that 'creativity' is not something we do but something we are. We were made at a word from God and then reborn by his Spirit in the name of Jesus. We bear the hallmark of the Creator God by being creative people, and one of our lifelong aims is to explore how we can best give Him worship and praise using all the gifts He has given us.

This Unit is about communicating the whole of God's good news to our children. We must not be attempting to reach only a child's mind, but their whole person – and to look for a whole-hearted response. Let us release children's creativity, and enjoy the results.

The creator within you

Is this how you are feeling?

> My reaction to the opening pages of this Unit have been disturbing. I had never realised before how unenjoyable this kind of activity is to me. I felt really tense, and even though there was no-one there watching me, I was angry that someone had set me these tasks.

> I have never enjoyed making things and at school I always felt most at risk in an art and craft lesson. We had a teacher who was a professional painter and we never did anything except use paint. Some of the other classes used clay and made junk models and I often thought I would have liked to have a go at those.

> The worst part was that, although I knew as she explained it what we should do, I couldn't do it! I also knew that I would be teased and ridiculed by the people who could do it. Awful – to know right from the start that I was going to fail!

> It makes sense though – this stuff about Genesis and having the Creator's likeness is something which appeals to me. Maybe I should aim for an attitude of – 'I may never be satisfied with the results, but I'm going to thoroughly enjoy playing around with this stuff'.

When we are getting involved in creative activities with children, it is important to know our own feelings about 'mess'. We each have a different pain threshold when it comes to mess.

- Some of us are neat, sophisticated and love beautiful things. We struggle with the necessary disorganization while creativity takes place.

- Some of us like order and beauty but, not being sophisticated, can cope with the mess in the cause of art and craft.

- Others of us simply do not care what mess is made, and seem not even to see the chaos. The result is all that matters to us.

In all of these cases the children we work with can produce some lovely, creative things. We all need to recognise our own natures and realise how different we are from others and how our own responses influence the experience of the arts our children have.

If you look at something which is not perfect and feel really disturbed by the 'faults' in it, then art and craft with anyone will disturb you too. Part of the process of exploring the arts is that something can always be bettered. The only perfect creation is made by the perfect Creator – and even that creation is always developing and on the move.

Responding to beauty

Another area of self-knowledge is how we react to beauty. As you look at the world around you and see lovely things – in creation, architecture, the performing arts and so on – how do you react?

Do you want simply to sit still and look or listen? Or do you want to express a response – take a photograph, sketch a picture, write a poem, talk about it to a friend, dance for joy?

None of these is a better response than the other, but we need to get to know ourselves so that we recognise and respect different reactions in children. Men may struggle more with their connection to artistic responses, and need to work this through and recognize the difference between practical 'jobs' and creative responses.

It is important that we understand that expressive response properly. If we dance down a hillside of buttercups, we are not auditioning for the Royal Ballet but responding to a moment of beauty when the air, the lighting, the place and the colours seem to demand a response! Our response is part of the beauty of the hillside, not something to evoke a response in someone else. The two are different and separate.

We respond to God's beauty as part of our worship, but at times that response can also communicate the beauty of what we have experienced to others – then they worship God too.

If you were given a choice of a creative gift for you to enjoy, which would you choose to receive?

To sing

To dance

To play an instrument

To design a Powerpoint

To wave banners

To create actions for a song

To write poetry

To read poetry

To paint

To sketch

To write a letter

To draw cartoons

To take photographs

To

To

To

To

To

Take a photograph of some expression of your creativity – a cake you have made, some flowers in a pot, a newly painted bedroom, a table laid ready for a meal with friends. Paste it in here:

What expression of creativity has given you the greatest pleasure and satisfaction?

Your image

Take a square of aluminium foil and hold it firmly to your face so that the imprint of your face is imposed on it. Gently lift it off your face and pin it up somewhere. It will be a picture of a creative person made in the image of a Creator God – and therefore made for creativity!

Creativity and learning

The use of the creative arts in school education is not simply about 'learning about art' or even acquiring the skills that the artist uses. Such learning is a part of education and can in itself be an inspiration. But schools recognise that the arts give children the opportunity to say how they feel about an issue or to express their feelings by entering into the way someone else has expressed theirs. In this way children are helped to experience the education process at a deeper level.

There are many useful resources in schools and churches which encourage leaders or teachers to work with children looking at 'old masters' based on Biblical themes. This not only stimulates creativity, but introduces children to the messages hidden in artistic responses.

A child listens to an amusing poem about how an adult poet remembers their maths teacher. As a result they might start to express how they feel about one of their own teachers – perhaps in a poem or in a list of words to a rap beat. Until then their feelings about that teacher may have simply produced a dislike of their subject or an aversion to short people with loud voices. But suddenly the whole issue can be unpacked – and there may be a much happier pupil as a result.

> ## Bear it in mind
>
> *We remember:*
> * *10% of what we hear*
> * *50% of what we see*
> * *60% of what we say*
> * *90% of what we do*
>
> *Being creative is a way of combining these ideal ways of learning.*

......and in church?

If only our churches took such a positive attitude! Some sections of the church are more open to the creative arts than others.

* You may worship and serve in a church where expression of thought and feelings through music, banners, drama, dance, poetry, visual images and song are encouraged and such gifts are grown.

* You may be in a church which encourages responses and prayers that are physical.

* You may be a member of a congregation which celebrates the gifts and skills of the 'great masters' of the past, but treats with disdain modern artistic expressions of faith.

Whichever is true for your church, the children in your church (and children outside the church in the local community) will be used to using the arts in their education. The church must find a way of welcoming and understanding this form of expression of their children's faith and beliefs – and of their doubts and fears.

The trouble is that adults in the church find it hard to fail, or make a mess in church. This is partly because we want to give our best for God, but partly because we don't want to risk failure in public – we will cringe every time we remember it! But expression of deep feelings through the arts does not produce 'perfect' results. There is only one Perfect Creator, and we reflect His character not by creating nothing (lest we should make a mistake) but by creating something, however flawed or limited that might be. We are never more like our Creator God than when we respond to the urge to be creative!

The expression of faith through paint and dough, movement and words is important not just for a child being educated, but also for the rest of the church. Many adults have forgotten the joy of such expression, and will be able to enter more deeply into their own faith as they see what a child has produced to express theirs. We need to appreciate the creativity of others, and be careful how we respond and react to things which we don't understand or don't think are 'finished'.

In the arts there is a wonderful 'level ground' for us all. Everyone's contribution is valid – we are not sitting an exam! The time and place for such expression will depend on the type of congregation and the way it structures its life. But it is not appropriate for any of us to say, "Creativity is not for me because I can't draw, paint, dance, play." If we feel like this, this is precisely a reason why we need to enjoy the creative contributions of a child. In any case the child needs it, and has a right to opportunity for such expression.

Be practical

If we are to encourage and enable creative expression to take place in the whole-church setting, we need to make sure that the mess which inevitably surrounds it is well organised and within boundaries.

- Plan how you are going to cover anything that will not clean easily: a sheet of plastic stuck down right over the carpet and sealed down with sticky tape.

- Provide a bowl of soapy water set firmly on a chair of the right level, with a towel hanging over the back.

- Use some plastic carrier bags with the bottom cut out of them, for aprons.

- Ensure there are plenty of extra hands to cope with a crisis.

- Use a hair dryer to dry work more quickly.

- Provide a big surface to mount the finished results, for any who choose to use it.

- Don't let the craft activity take over from worship, teaching and prayer!

So think through the implications of what you will be doing before the event. Otherwise in the middle of the mess and the muddle, you will find yourself vowing, "We're never going to do this again!"

A bridge to outside

Excluding the creative arts from our church life also removes one of the most powerful bridges for children's evangelism. When children who have never been in a church before first come into a church setting, it is often the times of creative expression which enable them to engage with what is happening. It is in the creative activities of a children's or all-age group that relationships are formed, confidences shared, parents become involved (if only to visit the display), and – if the activities have been carefully chosen – Christian truth is illuminated and explored.

What creativity does

Creativity in ourselves and in those around us:

- influences our thinking
- helps us to define our feelings
- helps us to express our feelings
- helps us to understand the attitudes of others
- is an expression in our lives of God the Creator
- is part of our worship of God

Make a list of the children whose work you have retained or photographed, with their ages and any details which you noticed about them at the time – especially anything they said to you about what they were doing. Label each of the 'exhibits' or photos with this information.

Nine things to do

'The marks of personality – love, communication, and moral sensitivity – which are meant to sharpen as we are returning to communication with God, should lead to an increased rather than a decreased creativity.' (Edith Schaeffer)

How and in what ways has a process of growing creativity been your experience since you began to live the Christian life? How would such a growth in creativity affect your plans and expectations for the children in your group?

Outline five ways in which you could use the creative attitude to communication to which Edith Schaeffer refers, in a weekend for the whole church to celebrate the refurbishing of a room used for children's clubs.

Write a description of the way in which the life of the local school enjoys creativity. Include some detail of the way in which the creative work is introduced, executed and exhibited. What were your feelings as you watched children involved in these activities?

Make an appointment with yourself to enjoy your own creative nature – even if that is not something you would normally think much about. For example, buy a ticket for a concert, a ballet, or an opera, and allow yourself to get emotionally involved. (Avoid television, where we stay to some extent separate from the creative experience.) Feel the live impact of this art form.

Talk to someone who is into visual expression, or pay a leisurely visit to a local art gallery.

Take your camera out into your local community and capture frames of it on film.

Borrow a book from the library which gives you art and craft ideas recommended for use with the age-group you lead. Set aside an evening for trying them out with a friend. Make a list of what you will need well ahead of time so that you find the evening satisfying and fun. You could put the results up for the children in your group to see (scary...!). Make sure you mount them at child level and not at your own height. Be brave and listen to the comments children make – after all, they usually have to listen to what you say about their results whether they want your comments or not! Be honest enough to show every example and not just the ones which were successful.

Look back over the programme for your children's group over the last six months. List the ways in which you have enjoyed children's creativity and have encouraged them to enjoy it. Make another list of activities which you did not include but which would have been appropriate.

Read the narrative in Luke 15:11-32. Devise a way in which five children of the age of the children in your group could use the creative arts to explore its meaning. How could they then communicate the story as a contribution in an all-age service?

Tools of the trade

This Unit outlines ten key skills in the leadership of children, and helps you develop them.

Contents

Ten tools for child-craft

a) Speech

b) Narrative

c) Teaching the Bible

d) Providing choice

e) Organisation & planning

f) Music/audio

g) Drama/video

h) Discipline

i) Prayer and worship

j) Growing young leaders

Assignment

Ten tools for child-craft

This workbook has concentrated on who you are as a leader of children, because this is foundational – although many people ignore it. But of course leadership, like most other roles, is also something you do.

So here are ten key skills in the leadership of children. You may want to work through all ten, or simply choose skills where you feel you need to grow in your abilities. Either way, focus on acquiring greater ability in the skill – not just reading about how important each is!

To help with acquiring skills, we all need feedback from others. So as you work on each skill, try to think of someone whose skill in that area you really admire. Then ask them to give you feedback as they see you using that skill with children.

Feedback is more helpful when it is specific. So ask this person specific questions about your exercise of that skill. On the next page is an example of questions you could ask about how skilful you are in using your voice.

A way of life

Churches are often looking for children's leaders who already have the skills outlined here. But often it is more realistic to look for leaders who are the right sort of **people** for working with children, and then 'grow' in them the skills they will need for the job. So these are skills that you can encourage every new leader to work through when they join the team, whether as a helper or as a main leader. They then become a way of life – and a fun exercise for leaders to do together.

These skills are not just learnt and grown once, and then used for a lifetime. They are skills that grow – and need to grow – year by year. So helping new leaders to acquire these skills gives each established leader a nudge to do more work on the skills too. It's a bit like sharpening the blade of a knife, ready to be used even more effectively again.

a. Speech

Communication between people depends on words. We all talk so much! When people cannot hear or lose their voice, other ways have to be found to make words known and understood. Often we say too much out of nervousness and insecurity, and may need to learn to be quiet to let others speak or to allow space for thinking.

One of the most important tools in the trade of leading children is your voice. And if you have ever lost your voice when you were responsible for a group of children, you will know what an enormous handicap that is.

Voice questions

Is my voice low, moderate or high? Does this cause any problems?

Is my voice loud or soft? Does this cause any problems?

Are there ways in which I need to make my voice more interesting?

Should I try to change the speed/pitch of my voice, or use more frequent pauses?

Is the style I use suitable for my group – too chatty, too formal, etc.?

Is the tone of my voice appropriate for this group?

When I talk, have I any particular mannerisms that are unhelpful or off-putting?

What is the best thing about my voice, a strength that I could develop more?

If you are not sure about these questions ask someone to take a video of you while you lead the group, and look at it afterwards. You may be surprised at how many mannerisms you have!

But how skilled are you in using your voice? Your voice is a powerful tool, if you have learned to use it well. Using your voice is not simply about

- being heard (volume)

but also about

- being understood (diction)
- holding attention (speed, pitch, pause, etc.)

Reading a story out loud is a good way to assess your voice skills. You don't have to think about what to say and can concentrate on how to say it. Ask someone who reads well to listen to you reading, and to give you feedback on your skills.

- Define the size of the group you are reading to, and the size of the venue. The hardest task is to read to a small group in a large venue – something many people have to do each week, leading tiny groups of children in cavernous church halls.

- Try reading as quietly as you can, and notice what has to happen to your diction – you almost have to spit out the hard sounds.

- Then try to produce the loudest sounds you can without shouting, and notice what you have to do to your throat and neck.

- Read some of the story fast (choose an appropriate bit), and then pause and deliberately slow down the flow of the words.

- Think about whether you would speak to a group of children differently from a group of adults. If that's the case be careful that you don't sound patronizing.

The aim of all these things is to keep up interest in what you are saying. The creative use of your voice will make the information you are giving memorable, whatever the content.

b. Narrative

A lot of the Bible is in the form of narrative. It is telling us 'the story' of God's dealings with us. We also need to be able to communicate the story of God in our lives, and even for mature Christians that can be a challenge.

In leading children, we need to be able to re-tell the story accurately in our own words, in a way which communicates the same truth to our children. This is the skill of narrative. We will use voice skills in telling the narrative, but creating the narrative is a skill in itself.

The skill of narrative takes time, effort and a lot of practice. Many leaders fall into the trap of re-telling the story in a way which interests the children but does not convey the same truth as the original story. This leads to disappointment and confusion when the children later read the Bible story for themselves. If we use narrative well, our children will gain real satisfaction from reading the Bible for themselves in later years.

To do this, we need to ask:

- Why is this story in the Bible?
- What is the main point of the story?
- What is the context, and what needs 'translating' so the children can understand?
- What is the shape of the story – does the climax come half way through, or at the end?
- Are there words or phrases in the text which I want to use exactly as they are written in the Bible?
- Is there a phrase which I could use throughout the story as a theme or slogan?

- What will the children learn about God by listening to the story?
- What will the children learn about themselves as they listen to the story?
- How can I prepare the children for listening to the story and 'hearing' its message?
- How might children respond to the story – so what needs to happen when the narrative is finished?

Can you think of some questions, parallel to the ones on 'voice' on page 137, which would help someone give you helpful feedback on your narrative skills? Write them down here.

c. Teaching in the Bible

The Bible is more than its stories. And the truth of the Bible needs to be taught to children as a whole, not as a series of unrelated stories. Children are often left to make the links themselves, but this is unrealistic, especially for children with little Christian knowledge or understanding. We need to aim for a balance between giving children everything and forcing them to agree, and giving them so little guidance or explanation that they flounder.

The truth of the Bible is a big story which goes from creation in Genesis right through to the gates of heaven in Revelation. All the little stories fit into that big story. Children will only grasp the truth in the little stories if they have grasped the big story. And whenever we are telling the little stories to our children, we need to be aware of their place in the big story.

Scripture Union has produced a time-line chart for children's groups which helps communicate the big story, and where each small story fits into it. This is an essential resource, as it enables children to see the whole picture.

On page 142 is one telling of the 'big story'. Of course it is only one way of telling it, but use it to remind you of some of the major themes. Where you don't like the way it is told, think about how you would re-tell it. Then have a go at re-telling it in your own words, using your narrative skills.

Keeping the 'big story' in mind will also help you teach the parts of the Bible that are not narrative. These are important too, for our children as well as for us.

Look at Psalm 98. How would you teach this Psalm to small children?

Look at Ephesians 1. How would you teach this passage to small children?

These are not easy questions, but important ones if our children are to hear the 'big story' in all its richness.

The big story

The gospel is the story of a God who, at the beginning of time, made people who were like himself – they had minds which could think the way God thought, they had mouths which spoke the way God spoke, they had hands which did the things which pleased God, and they had feet which walked where God would want them to walk. So God and the people he had made were best friends – because you are best friends with those people who think like you, speak like you, and want to do the things which you want to do.

But one day the enemy of God whispered into the ear of one of the people God had made, and for the first time on this planet there was someone whose thoughts were not God's thoughts. Her hands reached out to do something that God had said 'You're not to do', and her mouth began to make excuses for what she had done. And the story ends in the Bible 'and that evening they heard the Lord God walking in the garden and they hid from him among the trees'. Their feet took them away from where God was. The Bible says that the gate of heaven slammed shut and death rippled down through all the generations onto all people.

Ever since that day, everyone born on this planet has struggled to think God's thoughts, have had mouths which do not speak God's words, have hands which do the very things which God has forbidden them to do, and their feet have a strong bias away from God. So to our minds, God had a problem – he could not change his laws because his laws reveal his own nature and that cannot change. But he loves the people he has made. He made them in order to enjoy their company and for them to enjoy his.

So God came to our planet himself. He was born a real baby. He learnt to crawl and toddle – he was a real child, a real teenager, a real adult. But his mind only thought God's thoughts, his mouth only spoke God's words. His hands only did those things which God would do, and his feet only went where God would go. And people hated him. They strung him out on a cross and they tortured him slowly to death. God's enemy thought he had won – and of course he did. Here was God on a cross – God dying! But death can only keep hold of those who have done wrong and Jesus had never done wrong. So he broke the power of death, he strode out from the tomb, he gave his disciples the shock of their lives and he has never died again since that day. He went back to heaven and left the gate wide open.

Since that day anyone can come to God for forgiveness – any of us of any age, or race, or creed, or background. And because Jesus died and Jesus lives again, God forgives us for the wrong thoughts we have had and the wrong words we have spoken, our wrong actions and the wrong places we have been. The Bible says that when God forgives me it is just as though I never sinned, so death cannot keep hold of me either. On the day when my family mourns my death, I will be more alive than I have ever been before. I'm on my way to heaven!

And in the meantime God fills me with his Holy Spirit and very patiently day after day he is teaching my mind to think God's thoughts, he is teaching my mouth to speak God's words, he is teaching my hands to do the things he wants them to do, and he is teaching my feet to go where he wants them to go. A wonderful story.

My re-telling

How would your re-telling of the 'big story' differ in
- content
- tone

from the big story outlined here?

d. Providing choice

A lot of the Bible is in the form of narrative. It is telling us 'the story' of God's dealings with us. 'Choice' is one of the key words in our society. We are all supposed to have choice about pretty well everything, and we may even have too much choice - look at supermarket shelves! Children today are used to having a lot of choice in their lives. Many will be used to having a huge number of choices in the home and at school. In our teaching activities with children, we are using quite a restricted curriculum – the truth about God as we find it in the Bible. But it is important that our children are offered plenty of options from which to choose their activities. How can we do that? Well, it is a skill!

When you look through the programme you are going to run for your children, ask yourself, "When will I give them choice, and what will the choice be?" Children who enjoy an element of choice within familiar programme patterns and boundaries will learn better and remain attentive for longer. You are likely to have a very limited number of leaders and helpers – perhaps only two of you for 16 children – so you will need to think hard about how you will safely cover the options you are offering. But the choice must be there!

- You might think of the choice in terms of 'where'. So you could offer a floor activity, a wall activity and a table activity. You could go outside or use a different space.

- You could offer a noisy activity, a quiet activity, a messy activity, and an on-your-own activity.

- In practical terms, you might want to offer two activities which children could clear up afterwards themselves, leaving you only one which is dependent on you to clear up!

Each option will be tied in with the big truth you want the children to think about. Everything is tied into that, because you only have your children for a short period each week, and you want every moment to count.

Offering choice can become very time-consuming to prepare for. So collect together the basic equipment and materials for the more obvious options. They are then all quite easy to offer each time. You can add more specialist activities when you have the time and energy, or more help with your group.

e. Organisation & planning

Leading children well is a lot of hard work. But it doesn't all have to be done at once. With good planning, the work can be spread out over a period of time. This avoids the last minute panic, and the sense of it being 'all too much'.

Some of the planning may be done for you. There are good published resources, telling you what you can teach each week of the year, and how to teach it for each age group. If you use these over time, make sure that the writers are not repeating stories too frequently – or leaving other good Bible material out. There is always a need to think things through, adapt to your own situation, and get materials ready.

But there are other things to plan and organise well ahead of time:

- which leaders are going to be there on each occasion?
- which leader is going to be responsible for which part of the programme?
- which events need parental permission?
- which events need extra adult help, and are there suitable adults?
- can you make a display of children's work?
- have you booked meetings with other leaders to prepare and pray?
- what on-going training do the leaders need and how they will get it?
- what space and special equipment do you need?

f. Music and audio

Children respond to music. Rhythm is a fundamental part of their lives. It's difficult to imagine anyone leading children and not using music as a tool in some form or another.

It may be that you yourself are not naturally musical. But music is strategic in communicating with children, and essential in helping them to worship. It is therefore important to learn to use this tool in whatever form you can.

Music to listen to

It is hard to keep up with the constant flow of new songs and tunes on the market for children. But you can do a lot with an ordinary CD player and a few CDs with a mixture of music. There are many good songs and songwriters who are producing relevant and helpful songs, so there's no need to rely on the old trite ones!

- Use a song to set a theme for your club.
- Use some music after a story, and ask the children which of the characters in the story the music reminds them of.
- Play some quiet instrumental music while you set the scene for a story, to calm them for prayer time, or simply to set the scene as they arrive.

Music to make

Your children will often be more confident about making music than you are.

- The smallest child can learn to pick up their instrument and play it at the right time – and even to lay it quietly down on a folded blanket or cushion again.
- Simple percussion instruments can make sound effects for the different happenings in a story you are reading.
- If you use puppets, the children can make sound effects to go with the action.

Music to move to

Younger children dance and move to music unselfconsciously – and become the people in their imaginations. As they get older they are less likely to want to dance, but girls in particular will know dance routines to pop songs. Some children will use dance movements in their worship to God, while others will prefer to use movement dramatically in a story. Leaders need to join in, otherwise the children will feel they are performing.

Notes

g. Drama & video/DVD

As you have observed children in school, particularly in the playground, you will have seen how fertile their imaginations are and how readily they step into someone else's shoes. Drama is the structured way of doing this. It is often seen only as a form of entertainment, but drama is a tool you can use to lead children towards a living experience of God's truth, by encouraging them to enter into it in their imaginations.

How did Elijah feel on Mount Carmel?

Of course, you can tell the children what happened and how you think he felt, but as they enter dramatically into what happened, they will tell you how Elijah felt. And since Elijah was obeying God and fulfilling a lonely obligation to worship Him, they will be entering into a profound experience.

How did Peter feel when he had denied knowing Jesus and run away?

As they sit behind the curtain or in a dim corner of the room behind a chair on their own, they will come to conclusions about this which may make your own thoughts seem quite shallow.

You can also use drama which has been produced on video or DVD. Be familiar enough with the film so you can pause it quite frequently and ask "What do you think might happen now?" "What is he going to say next?" "How do you think she is feeling at the moment?" Beware of playing too long a clip without some leading questions and discussion.

h. Discipline

As you have read through these skills, the word 'discipline' might just have come into your mind. This is a difficulty many leaders experience. Children come to church groups with very different experiences of acceptable behaviour, and your expectations may be completely different from theirs. They will have gained their understanding from school, from other clubs, and from home. Strange as it may seem, children need clear boundaries for behaviour in order to feel safe.

- Draw up some ground rules with your group, which both they and you think are reasonable. Children will be used to doing this at school. If they have a hand in setting the rules they have 'ownership' and are much more likely to follow and enforce the rules.

- Make sure that parents and the church leadership are aware of the ground rules and the sanctions if children do not work to keep them.

- Display the ground rules where everyone can see them.

- Make sure that all the leaders understand the rules, the levels of acceptable behaviour, and the sanctions for children who test the boundaries. Refer back to the rules occasionally.

Children who are sitting around bored and unoccupied will tend to fill the vacuum with some activity. So think through your programme, and have equipment ready. Especially think through the beginning and end of each session. Reasons for poor behaviour:

- Not enough leader interaction with the children
- Dull, boring and predictable programme
- Lack of rules, or enforcement of those rules
- Challenging children who have difficult life experiences
- Fear of upsetting children or turning them away

'If the message of God is worth listening to, then no child has the right to stop another hearing it'

i. Prayer and worship

As leaders, we want our children to enjoy God. Prayer and worship in our groups is an important part of this. Many children have their first experience of communicating with God in your group time. From there they will gain the confidence to pray at home on their own.

- Help children to listen to God, and to put what they hear into words.
- Make sure that the prayer and worship does not get squeezed out of your programme by the craft activity or games!
- Explain prayer in a way that doesn't make it sound like a wish box or a one-way communication system.
- Explore different ways of praying – using music, candles, silence, movement, words.

So start slowly, try one thing at a time, and if it 'goes wrong', ask yourself:

- what had I expected to happen?
- why was I disappointed?
- how could I do it again differently?
- when will I try that again?

The book *Children CAN Worship* by Nick Harding (Kevin Mayhew, 1999) may help you think through worship with children in more detail.

j. Growing young leaders

Many churches use teenagers to help in their children's groups. This might be because:

- there aren't enough adult leaders.
- the church is committed to involving young people in ministry from an early age.
- there are teenagers who like being with children.
- there is no church-based group for teenagers to join, and this involves them.

Teenagers deserve their own activities, and churches should have a strategy for children's work which does not rely heavily on teenagers. But there are some teenagers who really want to learn about leading children, and some churches would have nothing for their children if their teenagers were not generous with their time.

So here are some guidelines for using teenage help:

- Listen to their ideas for the group and take them seriously.
- Involve them in planning meetings as a full member of the team.
- Spend time with them each week, so they know what is happening and they learn to prepare and to pray.
- Encourage them to exercise leadership. They could start with running a craft activity or a game; later they can learn to pray with the children.
- Ask them about their own faith, and how they respond to what is being taught in the group. Be ready to share your own faith with them, and your own feelings about what is going on in your group.
- Come to some kind of 'contract' about what is required of them and what they will gain from you. Are you asking them to come every week? Should they let you know if they are not coming? Is the church going to pay for them to have some training? Is this arrangement for the term, for a year? How will they tell you when they need to stop because of the demands of school etc.?

Assignment 7

If you are studying this course with a tutor you must do this assignment.

Reflections on practical and creative skills

Focus what you have learnt from units 8 ands 9 by writing a reflection outlining the practical and creative skills you feel you bring to the task of leading children and the skills you want to develop in order to do it better. Write about 500-800 words.

Send the completed assignment to your tutor for marking by post or email.

Being a leader

This Unit explores the meaning of Christian leadership and encourages you to develop such skills and attitudes, both in yourself and in the children you lead.

Contents

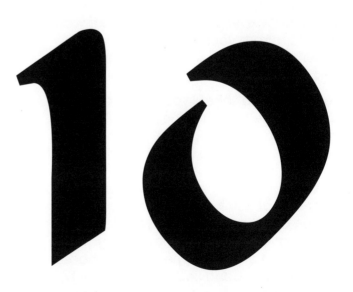

Born to be king?

Are leadership qualities embedded in our personalities and character from the beginning of our lives? Is the ability to lead something which some people 'just have', and others don't?

And no matter how much leadership potential we may 'naturally' have, how can those leadership qualities be grown and nurtured?

The preparation for this Unit is again to look both at children and at ourselves. Observe the phenomenon of leadership in children, and look at the evidence of your own life.

The second experience in particular will be more beneficial if you complete it in partnership with someone else, since the signs and qualities we are looking for are subtle and can be hard to detect and analyse. This need not be someone who is doing this course with you.

Chiefs......
......and Indians

The first piece of preparation is to observe how children take 'leader' and 'led' roles in the context of the school playground. If you have observed this kind of thing before, you can just reflect on that experience; but even so it would be good to refresh your emotional memory – and perhaps notice things you haven't noticed before.

Before you go into school you will again need to approach the headteacher officially, giving your reasons for your proposed visit and the nature of the course you are doing. If it is some time since you experienced being in a playground, you may need to ask to make two visits so that you have time to get used to the unique atmosphere before you start to do your observation. Lunch playtimes will give you a longer period of time. Some schools choose pupils to manage behaviour, befriend lonely children, or act as 'playground peacemakers'.

Taking photos may again be helpful. If want to do this, again ask beforehand so everyone is clear what you are doing and why. If this school-based observation is a problem do as before; that is, visit another church, an after-school club, or another suitable activity.

Here is a suggested outline for getting the most out of this experience:

Wander around the playground, preferably without a 'companion' (although with younger children you are bound to collect one or two).

Pick out in your mind two or three places where a group of children are playing together.

Observe these one by one, spending time standing to one side as inconspicuously as possible but where you can still see and hear properly.

Ask yourself the questions below and, when you get home, write down the impressions you have had about each of these two or three situations. Use the questions as an outline and add any further information which comes to mind. If you took photographs, you can add these to the description.

Who is in charge of the game?

Is their leadership disputed by anyone?

How do they maintain their leadership role?

Do they keep the game together successfully or do some people wander off?

Is there at any time a successful bid for different leadership?

Looking back

To look at the growth of leadership skills and character in your own life I suggest you construct a pleated person like this:

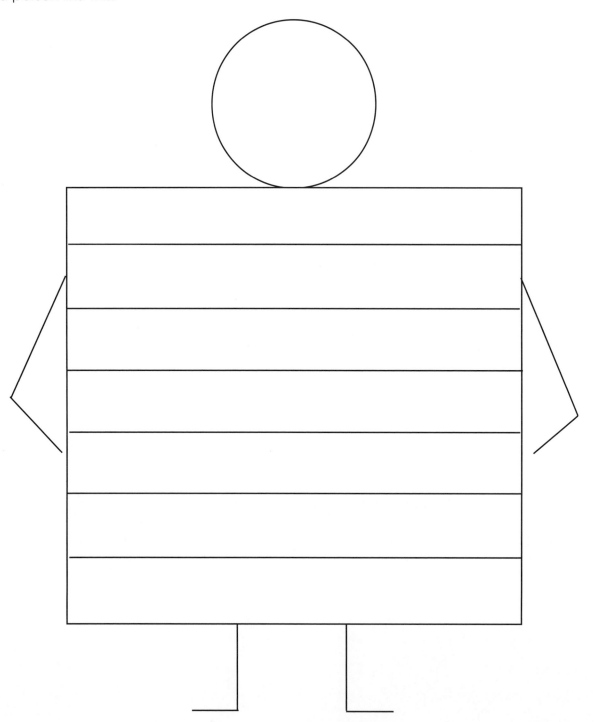

Working with someone else, talk through your life from its beginning, thinking of any way in which leadership has been grown in you by events, people, and as specific spiritual gifts. The tendency is to assume that this process only began when you were in your mid-teens at the earliest, but make sure you start from the beginning. For example, when you played with others as a child who did the organizing, and who did the following? Encourage your companion to prompt you with questions about your earliest years, because you are likely to find that some of the groundwork for growing you as a leader was done even before you started school.

Remember that a tough experience can make you strong, and when you are strong others are likely to look to you for leadership. Also, an experience of affirming love gives you confidence, which in turn causes others to look to you for leadership. Try to isolate experiences of these kinds.

As you pinpoint times when leadership was grown, fill in one of the pleats on the 'person' you have made, so that the person grows! Put them in chronological order from the neck downwards. Resist the urge to write them in large letters (because you're worried there won't be many examples...) because you will find that once you start, the list will grow at an amazing rate and the space will soon be gone.

God grows leadership in our lives in a thousand ways. When we take the time to recognise it, we will start to be excited by the prospect of that process happening in the lives of children in our groups now. When that happens we will start to see ways in which we can work with God in this amazing work.

Notes, or draw the person again

Just one step ahead

If a large group is on a demanding walk, the best person to follow is the person just one step ahead of you on the path. It is hard for everyone to keep their eyes on the group leader.

Hopefully the person just in front is in turn following other footsteps, and so we all end up following the one at the head of the line who knows the terrain and the ultimate destination.

In life too, the person you can best follow is often the one just ahead of you. The game 'Follow my Leader' is a good illustration; one person does in fact lead the whole line around the room, but each person is simply attached to the person just in front of them.

'Leadership' is a word which causes strong reactions from people. It can sound a heavy, official word with unpleasant overtones of authority and discipline. In fact the leadership role – in the best use of the word – is a role common to most people. There is a sense in which each one of us is a leader – we are followed by at least some others.

Leadership is a place of influence and effective relationship. It is a role which is exerted by powerful cult figures, but it is also one filled by close friends and relatives. Leadership in fact comes in a wide variety of shapes and forms!

Hezekiah

Look at the character of Hezekiah in 2 Kings 18-20. No-one reading the story handed down through history will see him as an example of a courageous and valiant king; Hezekiah ends up winning a war at the end of chapter 20 – without ever fighting a battle. But he is an encouraging example of how to lead others from only one step ahead!

In 2 Kings 19 Hezekiah is living in a capital city under siege. He is as smelly, thirsty, hungry and exhausted as the rest of his people. Hezekiah knows the reputation of the enemy, Sennacherib (2 Kings 18:9-12), because he had already taken many cities in the north. He has just made a very weak response to Sennacherib's aggression into the southern kingdom of Judah (2 Kings 18:13-16).

But Hezekiah puts his trust in God and in fact he does act as a strong leader – in three ways:

- by giving his people common-sense advice (2 Kings 19:36)
- by facing God with the reality of the situation (2 Kings 19:15-19)
- by facing the enemy with God's power, in the prophecy of chapter 19.

Hezekiah was only one step ahead of his people; but he led them through to victory with great success and brought honour to God.

Notes

Jesus

Not all leaders are like Hezekiah and we should not expect all Christian leaders to fit into one picture. The character of Jesus gives us a very different leadership picture. We can see this in Mark's Gospel:

Jesus prepares himself for a strong leadership role (Mark 1:1-13)

Jesus summons those he wants to follow him – his team (Mark 1:14-20)

Jesus is established as a leader of authority (Mark 1:21-28)

… and of supernatural power (Mark 1: 29-34)

Born of God and in touch with Him (Mark 1:10,35, 2:1-12)

And so Mark's gospel continues for 16 chapters. Look through the Gospel, picking out the leadership traits, and form a picture in your own mind of the kind of leader Jesus was.

Notes

Leadership styles

Hezekiah and Jesus are only two examples of a whole range of people in the Bible who led others. You will fit into that range at some point or other. It is important to see the kind of leader you are. In your role you not only lead children (and possibly other leaders in the team), but you are growing leadership skills in the children in your group.

Here are three leadership types. In a very simple form they show a range of possibilities. Each offers different strengths and weaknesses, different approaches to success and failure, different reactions to disagreement or frustrations.

1. The Strong Natural Leader

This person is full of ideas and eloquent in expressing them. They do not have much patience with people who do anything other than follow them, and they cannot understand why anyone should disagree with them. In fact if someone disagrees with them, they are likely to assume that the other person has simply not understood. To them, their ideas seem obvious, and when faced with an alternative they will often simply repeat their own idea again. These leaders are likely to have very high standards which they set for themselves and for others.

It is often easier and more effective in a group to let this person take the lead, although their emphasis will be always on getting results – not on process or people – and they will need a good pastoral person to work alongside them.

2. The 'Just Filling the Gap' Leader

This character is the one who has very little appetite for being a leader – perhaps finding it too lonely for a gregarious nature, or too restricting if it includes administration and pastoral care. These people become leaders either when someone else exerts pressure on them to take the role, or when the ultimate aim of the task is part of their personal vision and they do not want it to fail. The rest of the leadership package seems therefore worth accepting. These leaders may find the whole experience draining and painful.

If pressure has been exerted unwisely to persuade this kind of person to lead, there will be considerable support needed from others to keep such a leader buoyant and optimistic. This is when the team needs to work well.

3. The 'Such a Good Team' Leader

Such a person takes on the leadership of a group of people who seem gifted and energized for the job. They see their role as doing the basic, mundane work in order to free up the time and energy of those more gifted than themselves. Their emphasis will be on encouragement and team-building, on the basis that a united team is more productive than the sum of its parts. They will take pride in how the team develop and grow, but not want praise themselves.

Notes

Leadership in the church

I say 'leadership'. What do you hear? What kind of leadership immediately springs to your mind?

There are many different kinds of leadership, but each of us will have experienced particular models of it. We may have learned that leaders have to be ordained, or men, or dynamic, or mature. These will have shaped our expectations of others in leadership, and (more important) they will also have shaped roles which we will be trying to copy.

In fact there are three things which influence the kinds of leaders we are:

> The way you have experienced leadership will influence the type of leader you are trying to be.

> The type of personal characteristics you have will form the type of leadership qualities you are able to bring to the role.

> The way the Holy Spirit works in and through these natural means adds a third dimension to the equation.

Evaluating yourself

So what kind of a leader are you?

> Look at what your experience of leadership has been. Who have you followed most closely, and what sort of leadership have they role-modelled for you?

> Look at your personality and characteristics. What sort of leadership role are you most likely to be able to fill, out of the examples already mentioned?

> Look at the work of the Holy Spirit in your life. What gifts or strengths is God growing and using in you? What gifts have you not used for a while that need re-discovery?

All of these will help us to see the sort of leader we are and are becoming. To reflect on the last two in particular, you will need the help of a good friend or another leader – someone who will ask you the difficult and personal questions. You may also want to be taken through a personality profile to give you fresh insights into your personality traits.

Notes

Evaluating the church

It is important to recognise this variety in leadership styles and roles if the church is to function as it should.

There is a dearth of leadership in the church in our time, at every level and in every kind of work. The church will always have members – it offers a combination of support relationships, corporate goals and a sense of identity, which in themselves attract people. But such 'belonging' is not the whole spiritual aim of the church – this is not the fulfilment of the great commission. For the church to be more than a centre for social life and good works, we need good quality leadership.

So why are leaders so hard to find? One reason is that the church has used stereotypes in its models of leadership.

Stop for a moment and write down a list of words you would use to describe each of the following roles.

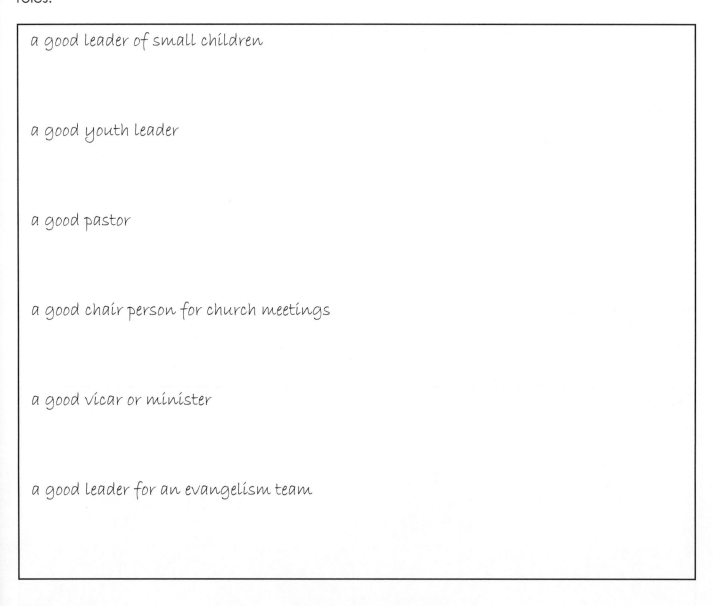

a good leader of small children

a good youth leader

a good pastor

a good chair person for church meetings

a good vicar or minister

a good leader for an evangelism team

If everyone who fulfils a leadership role in your church fitted the description you have listed of your vicar or minister, it would be a weak team! It would be weak and impoverished because each person would have the same strengths – and weaknesses! We need variety to make a strong leadership team. The task of the church is also very varied and requires leadership of many different kinds. We need to move away from thinking that the vicar or minister is the leader, and accept that he or she is one of a number of leaders.

The same is true of the children's leadership team. And the church needs to start looking with different eyes for potential leaders.

Ministering in a tired society

Our world is becoming ever busier and more demanding in the workplace. By the end of a working week people have no energy or creativity left – as research on family life and marriage relationships show.

Christians who exercise leadership responsibilities in their everyday lives find that they don't have the energy and appetite to exercise these in the church community too. They come to church because they want to receive the injection of spiritual life and healing which will resource them to go back to another gruelling week at work. They want undemanding worship and an anonymous place in the pew. They want the opportunity to sit back and let 'church' happen to them.

In our post-modern culture many people who come to church see themselves as consumers, and will only attend if they feel that they can gain from it. Membership and long-term commitment to a club, group or church is in decline as people pick and choose what they do, who they meet with and how they spend their time.

Big churches become bigger as people realise that they provide better opportunities for anonymity. But such churches have an ever-growing crisis of leadership as the balance between the servants and the served shifts disastrously. This is understandable, but the church is floundering without adequate leadership – and nowhere more so than in its work with children.

Washers and washees

To compound the problem, the church has propagated a poor definition for leadership. Whichever of the three types of leadership a person fits into, leadership is about service.

Try a simple exercise. Read John 13 with a friend. Collect together a bowl, soap, towel and some warm water. Now take time to wash each other's feet and dry them with the towel. This is best done in silence. Then write down words which describe both having your feet washed, and also washing the feet of your friend.

People expecting status and public recognition will find that leadership by God's definition has a hollow ring to it. They will often consider themselves 'not the type' for church leadership.

Many leaders in the church re-inforce this attitude – by not doing certain jobs, not asking for help, being all-capable and unquestionable. That is not the picture of leadership which Jesus painted as he washed his disciples feet and said to them "…You also should wash one another's feet."

> *The place of foot-washer and foot-washed is one role. Leadership is both. Leadership is to be served and to serve. It can be tiring, lonely, humbling and costly.*

Notes

New Testament teams

Look at the leaders Jesus chose (Mark 3:13-19). Make a list of the variety of strengths and weaknesses which come to your mind as you read through the list of names.

Compare the leadership list of the church in Rome (Romans 16:3-16). You probably won't recognise many of the names, but there is an exciting variety there.

And a child shall lead them

Good and effective leadership is not just born – it is also grown.

All leaders need training, motivation and encouragement to learn to use the gifts of leadership God has given them. This needs to be a regular experience – with no exceptions! Leaders who stop learning are dangerous people.

Ask yourself the following questions:

- What is the pattern of training leaders in your church? When is the next training session going to be?
- Is it clear that all leaders are expected at training events – or do people come if they have nothing better to do?
- Have the leaders been asked what their training needs are – spiritual, practical or educational?
- Is the church willing to pay for its leaders to attend training events and conferences?

Notes

I think it's likely that your answers will at best be unclear, at worst non-existent. Unfortunately this also influences the way we think about future leaders. We don't think clearly about training them either.

Despising youth

We have a lack of leaders in the church because each generation has thought that leadership is adult. It has only identified and grown adult leaders. But leadership gifts and skills are in people of every age, and if we only identify leaders in their more mature years, the church loses many of its young leaders through feelings of rejection and frustration. We will not end up in the future with leadership which has been carefully crafted and nurtured from childhood.

In our work with children we tend to talk about leaders (referring to adults) and members (referring to children). Yet as you observed children working or playing in groups you will have noticed that the leaders are not only the adults. Within any group of people of any age, some will naturally take the leadership role.

- In a situation of panic or indecision, certain people will step in and act.

- Where there is a strong suggestion made in a group, the other natural leaders present will question the suggestion or disagree with it.

- In a gap or lull of activity or conversation a leader will dive in to fill the space.

Leadership is not simply a job people are given to do, but a cluster of characteristics and attitudes towards both people and projects. If you look in any playgroup, playground or family meal table, you will see traits of the dynamics of leadership active amongst the children themselves.

- Some will exhibit leadership traits regardless of who is around – the natural leaders.

- Others will only do so if there is no-one else who will – the ones who fill the role if there is a vacuum of leadership.

- Still other children will become the servant to a group of energetic and exciting children and thereby get in on the action themselves.

The Spirit at work

When we spend time with children in the context of church life, another exciting dimension is observed – the Holy Spirit working in their lives as new gifts are given. These often set children on the course for leadership.

- The Holy Spirit may start to grow the gift of believing prayer in a child. A group of children are praying about something and other children may pray silently or briefly in single words or phrases – but this child will begin to pray coherently and with faith. They will be given a position of leadership by the other children in the group because they pray like that.

- Or the Holy Spirit may start to grow the gift of compassion in a child. They will then be the one who makes suggestions like, 'It would be good if we prayed for Sandy's mum' or 'I was

watching the Blue Peter Appeal – we could collect for that from our group, couldn't we?' That too is leadership, and other children will follow.

We must take note of leadership in young children and in teenagers, and use that leadership now in our groups. We need groups which have 'members' and 'leaders' of different ages – not just child members and adult leaders. The group is richer in experience and vision when this is so. You will be encouraged as an adult when you see the leadership gifts God is growing in the children in your group. And you will also be modelling true all-age church, where people of different ages learn from each other. Those gifts will not simply be for other children but will be used by God to lead you too! You will commonly find yourself listening to words of wisdom, and realising that God is directing you through the mouth of a child.

Growing young leaders

We can grow young leadership in many different ways.

If we want to see children as an integral part of the church we must learn to involve them fully and make the most of their leadership skills and gifts. The more children do and take responsibility for, the more they will have 'ownership', and the more likely it is that they will stay in church and become leaders in the future.

When you plan a programme and you identify the jobs which you and any other leaders might have, then identify which responsibilities you will give to children. Instead of asking for volunteers at the time, think about it beforehand and ask specific children; this way they can accept the responsibility seriously.

You may want a child to lead a small group on an outing or club night – tell them how many children, what the task will include, and what you will be looking for.

> "There will be six children in your group. You will need to find a dry place to sit within sight of everyone else and you will need to collect a tray of drinks and crisps when they are seated. Tell them where you are going. I will be especially concerned to see that the place where you have been sitting is clean and litter-free when we go back to the coach."

Then tell the whole group who the leaders are and who is in each group. Publicly thank them at the end and point out that you have noticed how organised the picnic was, that everyone had drinks and crisps at the right time, and that the picnic area was left tidy.

It is a very simple idea, and a task you could have done on your own, but by sharing the responsibility you have grown leadership skills in the new generation.

Or what about deciding the programme for the term. Have you ever asked the children in your group what they would most like to learn about from the Bible, or what their questions are about God? The Bible teaching can then address the agenda they have set. Or ask them about their preference for the pattern of being together – do they think there is enough prayer, singing, games, time for questions?

When you ask children to be involved like this, you are asking them to begin to take leadership responsibilities for the group.

Do it!

How could you involve children in the leadership of:

a church fun day?

an All-Age Service?

a strategy for home visiting the elderly?

an event raising funds for a charity or appeal?

a Holiday Bible Club?

a church magazine?

Ten tips for success

The projects children and young people can be involved in planning, preparing and praying for, cover such a wide variety that to make a list here would be impossible. It would include almost anything.

Here are ten top tips for growing leadership characteristics, skills and attitudes in even the youngest child.

Include the children in plans and preparation as young as possible.

If you watch a baby plan how to crawl to the electric plug the moment their carer answers the phone, or experience an older child playing off one adult against another, you will know that they are capable of brilliant strategy. So involve small children in the thinking behind your plans. So many children and young people see life as something which is done to them rather than something over which they have any control – and therefore responsibility. They will be used to 'owning' what happens to them, so make the most of it.

Include the children in praying about the plans.

Once children have realised that God is the real leader of the group, they are likely to remind adults to pray – to ask for his wisdom and for his blessing. Change the time for planning and praying so that children can be there. Give space for children to grow the skill of praying aloud, by restraining adults from long wordy prayers which will inhibit them.

Ask the children for their suggestions for what the overall aim of the group should be.

Listen to what is said and take it seriously. Be aware of the tendency of adults to be patronising to the young – it is not unusual for their simple statement to hit the nail on the head. Try to imagine how you would have relished this opportunity when you were a child, and how it could have helped you.

Work in pairs as you plan and prepare an event or programme.

In a mixed group it is usual for the adults to contribute and the children to listen. Break that pattern by working in pairs across the ages. A child and an adult, or a teenager and a child, working together, will each be able to make their own unique contribution but be mutually encouraging at the same time. At every age foster the ability to communicate, the ability to listen, and the ability to encourage.

Be there when the child does what you have prepared them to do.

It seems so obvious, but it can easily happen that at the very time when all this preparation, planning and praying comes into concrete form, the very person who has been most closely involved with the child and can give them the most helpful feedback is just not there! This is painful for the child, and should not happen.

When you give a child responsibility for part of the programme, make sure they know how their part fits in with the whole.

Their sense of satisfaction in using their own gifts will be so much greater –especially if you have asked them to do something quite small. As you use your leadership gift of communication to ensure they understand, they will not only make a good contribution but will also learn about leadership themselves.

Make sure that the children know how they connect with other people in the leadership team.

There are so many leaders who work in a vacuum – and we are not trying to grow that model! Make sure they know who is involved and what their role is, so that the rest of the team feels accessible to them in a way which might otherwise be difficult for a child.

Children who are given responsibility need to have one particular person to relate to.

It is important that a good relationship builds up between this adult and the child. This is the person they can turn to if they get stuck or need advice, and who will give them feedback on how well they have done. This feedback must not come unexpectedly or through overheard comments. The idea of feedback must be talked about beforehand, so that the child is told what the feedback will be about and will also see other experienced leaders receiving feedback in a similar way.

Give detailed feedback.

Don't just say 'Well done'. We all need more comment and help than that. Certainly comment like that immediately, or simply say 'I enjoyed that – did you?' But make sure that they know when you will meet them to talk properly about it. When you meet them, jot down on a piece of paper five things which were really good and one thing which could have been better.

Children taking responsibility need to have plenty of opportunity for trying things out and asking questions.

Making mistakes in public is one way in which people often find themselves vowing never to do something again! Whether you have asked them to lead the children's group with prayer, or chat to an elderly person in the congregation, or read in an All-Age service, go through the experience with the child, and help them to get the feel of what it will be like and what the reaction might be.

...and one big vision

When God loved the world so much he chose to save it, he sent a baby who grew into that place of leadership through an ordinary Jewish family. Allow God to stimulate your imagination to see what he can do through your growing of leadership traits in children. Babies are born every day – so are leaders. In all your pleasure, struggles and satisfaction of leadership of your children's group, you are growing children in their experience and knowledge of God. As they grow they also will be called and equipped to take the gospel to yet another new generation.

Too late?

Leadership takes time to grow and mature. If we want to have good adult leadership in the church in twenty years time, we need to start seriously to grow it now. Who will fill the staff roles in our churches then? Who will be members of regional and national decision-making groups in years to come, if we do not start to grow the necessary gifts in our children and young people now? To leave the recognition and growth of leadership gifts until adult years have been reached is short-sighted and ineffective – it not only impoverishes the church now but it means we are investing only in our own generation – and that will die with us!

Look at these Bible examples. They are useful role models of children in leadership: a king, a priest/prophet and a national saviour. They are all big roles entrusted to children by God, and then blessed by him to be fruitful and productive.

> *The roles of prophet, priest and king were ultimately fulfilled in Jesus who also came as a child, as prophesied in Isaiah 11:6 'And a little child shall lead them.' It was also Jesus who took a child as an example for his disciples to follow if they wanted to achieve greatness (Matthew 18) – a child setting the pattern to lead people to God.*

Josiah: 2 Kings 22-23

Someone has laid the foundation in Josiah's life (22:1,2)
   but has missed out the book of the law (22:8)
      he stands out against the enemy at last (23:4) – up until then other gods have been allowed.
        he uses other people – learns to delegate (22:2)
          but has vision
            and brings many people to obedience

Notes

Samuel: 1 Samuel 1-3

No knowledge of the Lord when called (1:1-5)
   discipled by Eli (chapter 3)
      not the finished article
         led to a growing knowledge of God (3:19-21)

Notes

Joseph: Genesis 37

Unattractive young man
  tactless
    went through tough times
      as a young leader, needed protection
        had to persevere
           saved God's people from complete disaster

*Leadership
is a child*

Notes

Assignment 8

If you are studying this course with a tutor you must do this assignment.

Leadership

Complete both parts of this assignment. Write about 1500 words in total.

1. Evaluate what kind of leader you are (see especially pages 158 onwards). This self-awareness of your style will be important in teaching others.

2. Describe how you will encourage and develop leadership both in the adults who assist you and in the children you serve.

Send the completed assignment to your tutor for marking by post or email.

Assignment 9

If you are studying this course with a tutor you must do this assignment.

Course file

Now send your whole course file to your tutor. Your tutor will not 'mark' every detail of what you have included, but it will enable him or her to see how you have engaged with the material of the course and grown through it.

THE LEADING CHILDREN TRAINING COURSE

If you would like tutor support in developing your ability to lead children, please complete the form below. We will then send you an Application Pack. You may photocopy the form if you prefer.

I am interested in the **Leading Children** training course.

Name
Address
Postcode
Telephone   Email

Please also send me details of the costs involved.

Please use the space below to tell us something about yourself: something about your background and why you are interested in doing this course.

Send the completed form to:

St John's Extension Studies
Bramcote
Nottingham NG9 3RL

Or send by FAX to 0115 943 6438

Telephone 0115 925 1117 for all other enquiries

www.stjohns-nottm.ac.uk

Certificate in Christian Studies
Strengthening the roots of your faith

The Certificate in Christian Studies is a practical course in applied theology, designed to equip people in every local church for ministry and mission. It is equivalent to one year of full-time study, spread over several years on a part-time basis. As a distance learning course, it is accessible throughout the UK and abroad.

A course to rely on

The CCS was established in 1978. Our current courses draw on over 30 years of experience – and it shows in the quality of our study materials, tutorial help, administration and other support. Thousands of people have completed all or part of the programme.

A course of Christian development

For many different kinds of people, the CCS has been a dependable way of developing their Christian learning and discipleship.

- Many have continued to serve God where they are – giving leadership to house groups, children's and youth work, and other roles in the church.

- Others have deepened their faith and witness in the world, living out a more thoughtful Christianity in the complexities of today's society.

- Others again have been enabled to progress to further studies, sometimes for formal ministries in the church.

A national course

The number of local courses on the Christian faith has mushroomed in recent years. Local resources are necessarily limited, and the experience of students on such courses varies a great deal. By centralising the development of resources and serving a much wider Christian public, the CCS has established itself as a training course of known quality, widely accepted in many church circles. This has also helped those who have subsequently moved from one part of the country to another.

The Certificate of Higher Education in Theology and Vocation is a university validated version of this course and can lead to a diploma or degree level qualification.

Leading Children is a **Faith for Life** publication in a series which includes *The Distance Learner, Fit for the Purpose (vocation), Something in Common (Anglicanism), God Thoughts (theological reflection), The Vital Connection (spirituality), The World Christian, Sustaining the Earth (Christian ecology)*. Watch out for new titles on our website.

For a detailed prospectus of distance learning courses and publications:

Phone:	0115 925 1117
Write:	St John's Extension Studies, Bramcote, Nottingham NG9 3RL
Fax:	0115 943 6438
E-mail:	ext.studies@stjohns-nottm.ac.uk
Web:	www.stjohns-nottm.ac.uk